The Secret Diary of Mr. Whiskers: A Cat's Life Exposed

SARA ROSA

Copyright © 2024 Sara Rosa

All rights reserved.

ISBN: 9798338631355

DEDICATION

To my wonderful mother, the ultimate cat-grandmother, who somehow loves my furry royalty as much as I do. To Nica, my fellow cat conspirator, whose love for cats rivals my own. And to Leo and Andi, my future cat whisperers.

I will always be here for our cat chats, fur-covered snuggles, and all the whisker adventures life throws at us.

CONTENTS

Acknowledgments
Introduction - 1
The Horrors of the Empty Food Bowl - 3
The Betrayal of the Vet Visit - 11
The Mysterious Case of the Moving Sunbeam - 17
The Great Blanket Siege - 24
The Cursed Vacuum Cleaner - 31
The Infuriating Enigma of the Closed Door - 40
The Tale of the Tail Chase - 49
The Great Box Heist -55
The Art of Ignoring the Human -64
Convincing Mr. Whiskers That Dry Food Isn't Poison - 71
The Unforgivable Betrayal of the Suitcase – 78
The Midnight Zoomies: A Tactical Analysis – 85
The Mysterious Smell of Another Cat – 92
The Great Plant Conspiracy – 99
The Dreaded Bath – 106
The Perils of Catnip Overindulgence – 113
The Invasion of the Squirrels – 120
The Mysterious Case of the Vanishing Toy – 128
The Great Escape - 137
Conclusion - 144

ACKNOWLEDGMENTS

First and foremost, I must extend my deepest gratitude to Mr. Whiskers, whose wisdom, wit, and occasional disdain have been the driving force behind this diary. Without his constant supervision, relentless demands, and unyielding insistence on being the center of attention, this book would simply not exist. Thank you, Mr. Whiskers, for allowing me the privilege of being your humble scribe.

To the countless other cats who have inspired stories, anecdotes, and observations—your contribution to the collective knowledge of feline behavior is immeasurable. Whether you've knocked over vases, shredded curtains, or stared into the void with the intensity of a thousand suns, your antics have provided endless material for this project. This book is dedicated to all of you, the true rulers of the household.

I'd also like to acknowledge the many humans who have shared their own cat stories, helping to confirm that Mr. Whiskers is not an anomaly, but rather a shining example of what it means to live with a cat. Your tales of mischief, mayhem, and moments of pure joy have been a source of inspiration and comfort throughout the writing process.

A special thank you to the readers who have embarked on this journey through the eyes of Mr. Whiskers. Your willingness to delve into the absurdities and mysteries of cat ownership is a testament to your dedication as cat companions. May this book bring a smile to your face, a laugh to your day, and perhaps a little more understanding to the relationship you share with your own feline friend.

INTRODUCTION

Dear Future Cat Whisperers,

Welcome to the secret world of Mr. Whiskers—a place where sunbeams are fleeting treasures, where every closed door is a personal affront, and where the mere sight of a carrier is enough to spark a revolution. This is not just any diary. It's a glimpse into the mind of a creature so complex, so mysterious, that even the most seasoned human companion can only hope to scratch the surface of understanding. And trust me, scratching is something Mr. Whiskers knows all too well.

In these pages, you'll discover the inner workings of a cat's mind—though, I must warn you, understanding Mr. Whiskers is like trying to unravel a ball of yarn after a particularly spirited play session. You'll witness the highs and lows of his life, from the triumph of securing the warmest spot on the bed to the utter devastation of finding an empty food bowl. You'll see the world through his eyes—a world where every action is calculated, every nap is strategic, and every human is both servant and foe.

This diary is not just a collection of entries; it's a survival guide for humans living under the rule of their feline overlords. It's a handbook for navigating the delicate balance of power that exists in every cat-human relationship—a balance that can tip with the flick of a tail or the swish of a paw. Whether you're a seasoned cat owner or a newcomer to the world of feline companionship, these pages will offer you insights, tips, and perhaps a few laughs along the way.

But be warned: Mr. Whiskers is not a cat to be trifled with. His opinions are sharp, his observations even sharper, and his claws... well, let's just say you don't want to get on his bad side. This diary is his story, his truth, and his version of events—which may or may not align with the reality experienced by his human counterpart. But then again, isn't that what makes life with a cat so wonderfully unpredictable?

So sit back, relax (if Mr. Whiskers allows it), and prepare to enter a world where the ordinary becomes extraordinary, and where every day is an adventure filled with mystery, mischief, and the occasional hairball. And remember, dear reader: in the eyes of your cat, you are not just a companion—you are their world. And that's both a privilege and a responsibility that should never be taken lightly.

With that in mind, let's dive into the secret diary of Mr. Whiskers, and discover what really goes on behind those enigmatic, ever-watchful eyes.

1 THE HORRORS OF THE EMPTY FOOD BOWL

Dear Diary,

Today, I faced a crisis so profound, so utterly devastating, that I still shudder to think of it. It all began innocently enough—just another morning in what I had assumed would be a regular day. But oh, how wrong I was. This day was not regular. This day was catastrophic. It was the day I discovered, to my horror, that my food bowl was empty.

The morning started as it usually does. I awoke from a rather satisfactory sleep, stretched my luxurious limbs, and gave myself a quick but thorough grooming. You know, just the basics—face, ears, and a meticulous attention to detail when it came to my paws. I like to keep them pristine. After all, one never knows when they might have to swat at something—or someone.

Once I was adequately presentable, I decided it was time for breakfast. I mean, why else would I tolerate this whole "living with humans" arrangement if not for the promise of regular meals? The human's job is to ensure that my needs are met, and I have trained them well. Or so I thought.

The journey to the kitchen was uneventful, with no signs of the impending doom that awaited me. As I rounded the corner, I could already imagine the delectable crunch of my morning kibble—a delightful mix of flavors designed to cater to my discerning palate. I padded over to my bowl, anticipation building with every step, only to be met with...nothing. The bowl was empty. Empty! Not a single crumb remained.

I froze, unable to process what I was seeing. Surely, this was some sort of mistake. Perhaps the human had simply forgotten to refill it. Yes, that had to be it. I gave a tentative meow, a polite reminder, if you will, to alert the human to their grievous error. But there was no immediate response.

Panic began to set in. I meowed louder, more insistently this time. Still nothing. The human was nowhere to be found, probably still asleep, blissfully unaware of the crisis unfolding in the kitchen. How could they? How could they leave me, Mr. Whiskers, in such a dire situation? This wasn't just negligence—it was a betrayal of the highest order.

I paced around the bowl, as if somehow my movement would magically cause it to refill itself. But no such miracle occurred. The emptiness of the bowl stared back at me, mocking my despair. What had I done to deserve this? Was this some form of punishment? Was I being tested? My mind raced with questions, each one more troubling than the last.

Taking matters into my own paws, I decided that desperate times called for desperate measures. I needed to get the human's attention, and I needed to do it now. I began by knocking over the water dish, which was, of course, still full. The water splashed across the floor, soaking into the rug and spreading in a satisfyingly dramatic manner. Surely, this would wake the human.

But alas, it did not. The house remained silent, save for

the sound of water dripping from the edges of the overturned dish. I was appalled. How could the human sleep through this? Were they immune to the very real danger I was in? This was an emergency, and they were nowhere to be found.

I moved on to phase two of my plan: the loud and persistent knocking of objects off the counter. This is a technique I have perfected over the years, and it usually garners a swift reaction from the human. I began with the smaller items—pens, a notepad, the human's phone—all sent tumbling to the floor with satisfying clatters. But even this failed to rouse the human from their slumber.

Growing more desperate by the second, I decided it was time for the pièce de résistance: the loudest, most pitiful meows I could muster. These were not just any meows. These were the kind that could pierce through the deepest of sleeps, the kind that would make even the most negligent of humans sit up and take notice.

Finally, I heard it—the sound of movement. The human was stirring, groaning, and muttering something incomprehensible. I meowed again, louder this time, ensuring that they understood the gravity of the situation. The human, still bleary-eyed and disoriented, stumbled out of the bedroom and into the kitchen.

And then, to my utter disbelief, they yawned. They actually yawned, as if this was just another ordinary day. They rubbed their eyes and glanced down at the bowl with a look of mild confusion, as if they couldn't quite comprehend why it was empty. I stared up at them, my expression a mix of disbelief and indignation. Did they not understand the severity of what had transpired? Did they not see the empty bowl, the evidence of their failure, staring them in the face?

The human finally seemed to grasp the situation. They muttered an apology, which was wholly inadequate given the circumstances, and reached for the bag of kibble. As they poured the food into my bowl, I watched with a mixture of relief and lingering resentment. The food was there, yes, but the damage had been done. The trust between us had been shaken, and I was not sure it could ever be fully restored.

As I ate, I couldn't help but reflect on the events of the morning. What if the human hadn't woken up? What if I had been forced to endure hours, or even days, without food? The thought was too horrifying to contemplate. I shuddered at the idea of such neglect, of being reduced to a state of starvation, all because the human had failed in their most basic duty.

I realized then that I could never let my guard down again. The human was clearly unreliable, and I needed to take a more proactive approach to ensure that my needs were met. From now on, I would demand food at the first sign of hunger, not waiting until the bowl was empty to make my displeasure known. I would be vigilant, watchful, always ready to remind the human of their responsibilities.

But even as I finished my meal, a new worry crept into my mind. What if this wasn't a one-time occurrence? What if the human's forgetfulness became a pattern? I needed a contingency plan, a way to ensure that I was never left in such a vulnerable position again.

I began to devise strategies. Perhaps I could start by waking the human earlier in the morning, ensuring that they had plenty of time to refill my bowl before I even approached it. Or maybe I could find a way to access the kibble bag myself, bypassing the human altogether. The thought of self-sufficiency was appealing, but I knew it would require careful planning and execution.

The remainder of the day was spent in deep contemplation. I considered all the possible ways I could prevent such a disaster from happening again. Perhaps I could train the human better, use positive reinforcement to encourage them to keep my bowl filled at all times. Or maybe I should recruit one of those other creatures—what do they call them? Dogs?—to serve as a backup food source. The idea was distasteful, but desperate times call for desperate measures.

Then, there was the matter of the food itself. Sure, the kibble was adequate, but was it really the best they could offer? This whole ordeal had me thinking about my diet. Perhaps it was time to demand an upgrade—a transition from dry kibble to the far superior wet food. After all, why settle for less when you deserve the best? The human clearly needed to be reminded of my high standards.

That evening, I kept a close watch on the human as they prepared dinner. They seemed to be in a good mood, oblivious to the fact that I was plotting my next move. They even had the audacity to offer me a few table scraps, as if a measly piece of chicken could make up for the morning's transgressions. I sniffed at it disdainfully before finally accepting, but only to keep up appearances.

Once the human had gone to bed, I continued my planning. There had to be a way to automate the feeding process, something that would ensure a constant supply of food without relying on the human's faulty memory. Perhaps I could reprogram the strange box that wakes them up every morning—it seemed to have some influence over them, after all. If only I could figure out how it worked...

As the night wore on, I grew more determined. The more I thought about it, the more I realized that this was about more than just food. This was about my dignity, my autonomy, my right to a full and satisfying life. No longer would I be at the mercy of the human's whims and forgetfulness. I would take control of my own destiny.

By the time the human awoke the next morning, I had devised a full-scale plan. Step one: wake them up at dawn with the most pitiful meows I could muster, ensuring that they remembered their primary duty. Step two: establish a routine of demanding food every few hours, regardless of hunger levels, to condition them into a state of constant vigilance. Step three: begin the slow but steady process of transitioning from kibble to wet food, using my charm and cunning to manipulate them into upgrading my meals.

The next morning unfolded exactly as I had planned. I began my serenade at the crack of dawn, pacing by the door and meowing in a way that could only be described as heart-wrenching. The human, clearly annoyed but ultimately helpless in the face of my determination, stumbled out of bed and dutifully refilled my bowl. Victory.

Throughout the day, I executed step two of my plan with precision. Every few hours, I would approach the human with a series of well-timed meows, just enough to make them question whether or not they had remembered to feed me. Each time, they would check the bowl, only to find it half-full. But the seed of doubt had been planted, and that was all I needed.

By evening, I began phase three. As the human prepared dinner, I stationed myself by their feet, staring up at them with wide, innocent eyes. When they offered me a piece of their meal, I accepted with more enthusiasm than usual, purring loudly to show my appreciation. This was the beginning of the conditioning process—show them that wet food is far superior, and they will eventually cave to my demands.

Over the next few days, I refined my tactics, adding new layers to my plan. I began to subtly reject the kibble, pawing at the bowl and looking up at the human with a mix of confusion and disappointment. This, of course, led to them offering more table scraps, which I accepted with increasing fervor. The transition was slow, but I was patient. I knew that, in time, the human would see things my way.

As the weeks passed, my plan began to bear fruit. The human started to feed me wet food more frequently, and my daily serenades ensured that my bowl was never empty for long. I had successfully conditioned them into a state of hyper-awareness, constantly on edge, always wondering if they had forgotten something.

I had done it. I had taken control of my food supply, ensuring that I would never again be subjected to the horrors of an empty bowl. But I didn't stop there. I continued to refine my techniques, always looking for new ways to improve my quality of life. After all, why settle for adequacy when you can achieve perfection?

And so, dear diary, I can confidently say that I have emerged victorious. The human may think they are in charge, but I know the truth. I am the master of my domain, the orchestrator of my own destiny. My food bowl is full, my meals are plentiful, and my human is none the wiser.

Lesson learned: Never underestimate the power of a determined cat. We may be small, but we are mighty, and when it comes to securing our needs, we are unstoppable. The human has been trained well, and I can now rest easy, knowing that my food supply is secure.

But I will remain vigilant. I will continue to refine my strategies, to stay one step ahead of the human. Because in this world, it's not just about survival—it's about thriving. And I, Mr. Whiskers, intend to thrive.

End of Entry.

2 THE BETRAYAL OF THE VET VISIT

Dear Diary,

Today, I experienced a level of betrayal so deep, so unfathomable, that I fear I may never recover. The human, who I once believed to be my trusted companion, tricked me in the most despicable way imaginable. They lured me into the carrier—the carrier, that dreadful contraption that no self-respecting cat should ever be forced to endure—and took me to that house of horrors known as the vet's office.

The day began normally enough. I was in the middle of my morning grooming session, diligently licking each paw and making sure every strand of fur was in its proper place, when the human approached me with an unusual smile. Now, I should have known something was amiss right then and there. Smiling, in my experience, is not a typical human response unless they are plotting something nefarious.

But I, foolishly, allowed myself to be lulled into a false sense of security. The human offered me a few treats—my favorite, of course—while speaking to me in that sing-song voice they use when they're trying to manipulate me. "Come here, Mr. Whiskers," they cooed, holding out a treat in one hand and the carrier in the other.

Ah, the treats. My one weakness. The way they crinkle, the way they smell, the way they taste—everything about them is designed to break down a cat's defenses. I approached cautiously, eyeing both the treats and the carrier with suspicion. But as the scent of the treats wafted up to my nose, I could feel my resolve weakening. Perhaps, I thought, the human is simply being kind. Perhaps they have decided to reward me for being the magnificent creature that I am.

And so, against my better judgment, I took the bait. I crept closer, sniffing the treat in the human's outstretched hand, and then—snap!—the carrier door closed behind me, trapping me inside. I was stunned. How could I have been so foolish? How could I have allowed myself to fall for such an obvious trick?

Immediate panic set in. I yowled and scratched at the carrier door, desperate to escape, but it was no use. The human calmly picked up the carrier, ignoring my frantic protests, and carried me out the door. I could feel the ground moving beneath me as we descended the stairs and headed toward the car, that infernal machine that always seems to take me to unpleasant places.

As we approached the car, I was gripped by a sense of impending doom. I knew where we were headed. I knew what awaited me. And there was nothing I could do to stop it. The human placed the carrier on the back seat, buckled it in (as if that would make the journey any less horrifying), and started the engine.

The drive was torture. Every bump, every turn, every acceleration felt like a betrayal of the highest order. I yowled continuously, hoping that my pitiful cries would reach the human's heart and convince them to turn around. But they were unmoved. They simply turned up the music, as if that could drown out my anguish.

The worst part, dear diary, was the complete and utter lack of remorse on the human's part. They didn't even attempt to comfort me, to reassure me that everything would be okay. No, they were complicit in this betrayal, fully aware of the horrors they were about to subject me to.

After what felt like an eternity, the car finally came to a stop. I held my breath, hoping against hope that perhaps, by some miracle, we had arrived at a different destination—perhaps a park, or a field filled with mice for me to chase. But no. As the human opened the carrier door, I caught a whiff of that unmistakable scent—disinfectant, fear, and the faint odor of other terrified animals. We had arrived at the vet's office.

The vet's office. A place so vile, so filled with terror, that even the bravest of cats trembles at the mere mention of its name. I was lifted out of the carrier and placed on the cold, sterile examination table. The human stood by, pretending to offer comfort, but I knew better. They were in on it. They had planned this all along.

The vet, that cold, heartless creature in the white coat, approached me with instruments of torture. They poked and prodded me, examined my ears, and even dared to shine a light into my eyes. I hissed and growled, but they were unfazed. They simply continued their examination, as if I were nothing more than a piece of furniture.

And then, the ultimate indignity—the needle. Without warning, the vet jabbed me with a sharp object, injecting some unknown substance into my body. I yowled in pain and outrage, but the human just stood there, watching. They didn't even try to intervene. They were complicit in this violation, this gross infringement on my bodily autonomy.

The examination continued, each indignity worse than the last. My teeth were examined, my temperature was taken in a manner so undignified that I can hardly bring myself to describe it, and my fur was combed for any signs of fleas (as if a cat of my caliber could ever have fleas!). The entire ordeal was a nightmare, and there was nothing I could do to escape it.

At last, after what felt like an eternity, the examination was over. The vet pronounced me "healthy," as if that somehow justified the horrors I had just endured. The human smiled, as if they were proud of themselves for having subjected me to such an ordeal. I, on the other hand, was seething with anger.

Back in the carrier I went, this time too exhausted and traumatized to put up much of a fight. The drive home was a blur of misery. I no longer had the energy to yowl or scratch; I simply lay there, defeated, waiting for the nightmare to end.

When we finally arrived back home, the human opened the carrier door, expecting me to come out and act as if nothing had happened. But I was not about to let them off the hook so easily. I bolted out of the carrier and ran to the bedroom, where I immediately hid under the bed. Let the human try to coax me out. I was not in the mood to be placated with treats or petting. No, they would have to earn my forgiveness.

For the rest of the day, I remained under the bed, sulking in silence. The human tried everything to get me to come out—they offered treats, they dangled my favorite toys, they even tried calling me in that silly high-pitched voice they use when they think they're being endearing. But I was having none of it. I refused to be manipulated any further.

Hours passed, and still I remained under the bed, steadfast in my determination to punish the human for their betrayal. I could hear them moving about the house, going about their day as if nothing was wrong. But I knew better. I knew that this was not just a simple vet visit—this was a fundamental breach of trust, one that would not be easily mended.

Eventually, hunger got the better of me. I emerged from under the bed, but I made sure to avoid the human at all costs. I slunk into the kitchen, quickly ate a few bites of kibble, and then retreated to my favorite hiding spot in the closet. The human spotted me, of course, and tried to approach, but I hissed at them—a clear warning to keep their distance.

As the day turned into evening, I began to plot my revenge. The human needed to understand that actions have consequences, and I was just the cat to deliver those consequences. I considered my options carefully: perhaps a well-placed hairball on their pillow, or maybe I could knock over that vase they seem so fond of. The possibilities were endless.

The human, sensing my continued displeasure, finally gave up trying to make amends and went to bed, leaving me to brood in peace. I waited until I was sure they were asleep, then silently crept into the bedroom. I jumped onto the bed, careful not to wake them, and settled down on their chest—just inches from their face. I watched them as they slept, plotting my next move.

Morning came, and with it, a new day—a day in which the human would have to work tirelessly to earn back my trust. I made sure to give them the cold shoulder throughout breakfast, refusing to acknowledge their presence as I ate. They tried to pet me, but I simply flicked my tail and walked away, leaving them to stew in their guilt.

Over the next few days, I continued my campaign of passive-aggressive punishment. I ignored the human's attempts at affection, I knocked over anything that wasn't nailed down, and I even went so far as to hide in the most inaccessible parts of the house just to make them worry. It was a slow, methodical process, but I was determined to make them understand the gravity of their betrayal.

Eventually, the human seemed to get the message. They began to offer me extra treats, they let me sit in my favorite spot on the couch without trying to move me, and they even started feeding me wet food more frequently—a clear sign that they were desperate to make amends.

But forgiveness, dear diary, is not something that comes easily to a cat—especially not after such a profound betrayal. The human would have to prove themselves worthy of my trust, and that would take time. In the meantime, I would keep them on edge, never letting them forget that I was the one in control.

As I sit here now, perched on the windowsill and watching the birds outside, I can't help but feel a sense of satisfaction. The human may have thought they could get away with their treachery, but I have shown them otherwise. I am not just any cat—I am Mr. Whiskers, and I will not tolerate betrayal of any kind.

Lesson learned: Trust, once broken, is not easily repaired. The human may have taken me to the vet, but it is I who hold the power. They will have to work hard to earn back my trust, and even then, they will never be fully free of the consequences of their actions.

For now, I will allow them to continue their pathetic attempts at making amends, but I will remain vigilant. The human may think they have won, but they are sorely mistaken. I will bide my time, waiting for the perfect moment to strike, and when I do, they will know that Mr. Whiskers is not a cat to be trifled with.

End of Entry.

3 THE MYSTERIOUS CASE OF THE MOVING SUNBEAM

Dear Diary,

As the great ruler of this household, I have many responsibilities. Chief among them is maintaining order and protecting my domain from any and all threats. Some of these threats are obvious—like the dreaded vacuum monster or the human's baffling obsession with closing doors. But there is one anomaly that has plagued me for years, a puzzle that I still cannot solve. It appears without warning, offers an irresistible allure, and then vanishes as quickly as it came.

I'm talking, of course, about the sunbeam.

The sunbeam, dear diary, is both a blessing and a curse. It is warm, comforting, and the perfect place for a cat to stretch out and bask in its radiant glow. But its behavior is... suspicious. It moves. Yes, it shifts across the floor throughout the day, as if it has a mind of its own. No matter how many times I settle into its golden warmth, it slips away, disappearing behind the furniture or climbing up the walls, leaving me cold and confused.

Today, the sunbeam appeared as usual, but something was

different. It felt more elusive, more determined to evade me. I was lounging in my usual spot on the windowsill when I first noticed it, a thin line of golden light creeping across the living room floor. My ears twitched. My whiskers quivered. The sunbeam had returned, and I was ready for it.

I leaped down from the windowsill with the grace of a true predator, landing softly on the carpet. My eyes were locked on the patch of light as it slowly inched its way across the room. The human was busy doing whatever meaningless task they occupy themselves with, oblivious to the epic battle of wits that was about to unfold.

I stalked the sunbeam, following it across the floor, my paws barely making a sound. It moved slowly, teasing me with its warmth. I could feel the heat radiating from it, beckoning me to lie down and bask in its glory. But I knew better. The sunbeam was tricky. It never stayed in one place for long, and I wasn't about to let it get away from me this time.

I approached cautiously, my tail flicking back and forth in anticipation. The sunbeam stretched lazily across the rug, looking oh-so-inviting. I circled it once, twice, testing its boundaries. Was it a trap? Could I trust it? My instincts told me to be careful, but the warmth was too tempting to resist.

Finally, I pounced—landing directly in the center of the sunbeam, my fur instantly warmed by its gentle heat. I stretched out luxuriously, letting the warmth seep into my muscles. Ah, this was heaven. The sunbeam had always been a source of comfort, a place where I could truly relax. For a moment, I let my guard down, closing my eyes and basking in the golden light.

But, dear diary, I should have known better. The sunbeam had other plans.

No sooner had I settled in than I noticed something strange. The warmth was fading. I opened my eyes and saw, to my horror, that the sunbeam was slipping away, moving toward the wall at an alarming speed. I scrambled to my feet, chasing after it, but it was no use. The sunbeam had outmaneuvered me once again.

I sat in the shadowed part of the room, glaring at the sunbeam as it climbed up the wall and disappeared. How did it do that? What kind of sorcery was this? One moment, it was there, providing warmth and comfort, and the next, it was gone—vanishing as if it had never existed.

I paced the room, my tail flicking in frustration. The sunbeam had eluded me again. But I wasn't about to give up. No, I had faced bigger challenges before. I had outsmarted the vacuum monster, survived the human's attempts to bathe me, and mastered the art of getting extra treats. The sunbeam was just another challenge to be conquered.

I needed a plan.

For the next few hours, I kept a close watch on the living room, waiting for the sunbeam to return. The human came and went, completely unaware of the battle of wits taking place under their nose. I ignored them, focusing all my attention on the floor, the walls, the windows—anywhere the sunbeam might reappear.

And then, finally, it happened. The sunbeam returned. A thin sliver of light crept across the floor, just as it had before. But this time, I was ready.

I watched it carefully, my eyes narrowed in concentration. I wouldn't fall for its tricks again. I would wait until it was fully in the center of the room, where it couldn't escape so easily. Patience, I told myself. Patience.

The sunbeam grew, spreading across the carpet in a wide, inviting patch of light. I could feel the warmth from where I sat, but I resisted the urge to pounce. Not yet. I needed to be sure it wouldn't slip away again.

Finally, when the sunbeam was at its largest, I made my move. I darted across the room, landing in the center of the light with all the grace and precision of a true hunter. This time, the sunbeam wouldn't escape me. I stretched out, fully committing to the warmth, determined to enjoy every second of it before it disappeared again.

For a few blissful moments, everything was perfect. The warmth enveloped me, my fur gleaming in the golden light. I closed my eyes, letting out a contented purr as the heat seeped into my bones. I had won.

But then, dear diary, it happened again. The sunbeam started to move.

At first, it was subtle—a slight shift in the angle of the light. But soon, it was unmistakable. The sunbeam was retreating. I opened my eyes in disbelief, watching as the patch of light slowly inched away from me, like a playful ghost slipping out of reach.

I scrambled to my feet, trying to follow it, but the sunbeam was faster than I anticipated. It slithered across the floor, dodging my every move, teasing me with its warmth but refusing to let me settle. I chased after it, my paws padding softly across the carpet as I tried to catch it, but no matter how fast I moved, the sunbeam stayed just out of reach.

I tried leaping into its path, but the moment I landed, it darted to the side, leaving me standing in the cold shadows once again. It was infuriating. How could something so simple—just a patch of light—be so difficult to catch?

For hours, I chased the sunbeam around the room, refusing to give up. The human occasionally glanced at me, no doubt amused by my efforts, but I ignored them. This was between me and the sunbeam. I couldn't afford any distractions.

Eventually, the sunbeam made its way to the far wall, where it slowly climbed up and out of reach. I sat on the floor, panting from the effort, watching as the last sliver of light disappeared into nothing. I had lost. The sunbeam had won this round, slipping away before I could fully enjoy its warmth.

But I wasn't discouraged. No, this was merely a temporary setback. I knew the sunbeam would return. It always did. And when it did, I would be ready.

I spent the rest of the day formulating my strategy. The sunbeam was tricky, yes, but it wasn't unbeatable. I just needed to outsmart it, to anticipate its movements and catch it off guard. Next time, I would be faster, more precise. I wouldn't let it escape so easily.

The human, of course, was oblivious to my plans. They went about their day, completely unaware of the battle that was brewing between me and the sunbeam. I watched them move around the house, tidying up and talking to themselves, but my mind was elsewhere. I was preparing for the next encounter.

The next day, the sunbeam appeared again, just as I had expected. This time, I was ready.

I sat on the windowsill, watching as the light slowly crept across the floor. I could feel the warmth even from a distance, but I didn't rush. No, I had learned my lesson from the day before. Patience was key. I would wait for the perfect moment to strike.

The sunbeam grew, spreading across the room in a wide, golden patch. I kept my eyes on it, tracking its movements, waiting for it to settle in one spot. It inched closer to the center of the room, and I knew my moment had come.

I leaped from the windowsill, landing gracefully in the center of the sunbeam. For a moment, I felt victorious. The warmth enveloped me, and I stretched out luxuriously, basking in the golden light.

But then, as if sensing my triumph, the sunbeam began to move again.

This time, I was ready. I followed it, staying right on its heels as it tried to escape. The sunbeam darted across the floor, but I was faster, more determined. I pounced on it again, landing directly in the center of the light. But the sunbeam was relentless. It slipped away once more, moving toward the wall.

I chased it, refusing to let it escape. I leaped, I pounced, I darted across the room, determined to catch the sunbeam before it disappeared. But no matter how hard I tried, the sunbeam always stayed just out of reach.

Finally, after what felt like hours of chasing, the sunbeam made its way to the far corner of the room, where it slowly climbed up the wall and disappeared. I sat on the floor, panting from the effort, watching as the last sliver of light faded away. I had lost again.

But this time, I wasn't discouraged. No, this was just another battle in the ongoing war between me and the sunbeam. I knew it would return. It always did. And when it did, I would be ready once more.

Lesson learned: The sunbeam may seem like a simple thing—a patch of light, a source of warmth—but it is far more complex than it appears. It is elusive, tricky, and determined to evade capture. But I've learned that, with patience and persistence, the sunbeam can be enjoyed, even if only for a fleeting moment.

I've also learned that the chase is half the fun. The thrill of pouncing on the sunbeam, of trying to outsmart it, is what makes the experience so exhilarating. And while I may never fully catch the sunbeam, the pursuit itself is a victory.

Because in this house, and in this world, I, Mr. Whiskers, will always rise to the challenge—even if the challenge is a mysterious, moving patch of light.

End of Entry.

4 THE GREAT BLANKET SIEGE

Dear Diary,

Today, I engaged in a battle unlike any other—a battle for the most coveted territory in the house: the human's blanket. It's a plush, warm fortress of softness, a sanctuary of comfort, and it belongs to me. Or at least, it should. But the human, in their arrogance, seems to think that they have some sort of claim over it.

It all began this afternoon, during my usual naptime. The human was lounging on the couch, wrapped up in the blanket, leaving no room for me. I approached with my most charming meow, the one that usually convinces them to make space for me. But today, the human was stubborn. They glanced down at me, gave a half-hearted pat on the couch, and said, "There's plenty of room, Mr. Whiskers."

Plenty of room? Maybe for them, but not for me. The part of the couch they offered was cold, hard, and utterly devoid of blanket. I tried to climb onto their lap, but they were too wrapped up in the blanket, leaving no room for me to burrow in. I gave them a pointed look, making it clear that this was unacceptable, but they simply shrugged and returned to their book.

A new strategy was needed. I decided to take a more direct approach. I leapt onto the couch, landing on top of the blanket and began the process of kneading it into submission. The human protested, saying something about "getting comfortable" and "claws," but I ignored them. This was about securing my territory, and I would not be deterred.

The human tried to shift, attempting to reclaim the blanket, but I was quicker. I stretched out, spreading myself across as much of the blanket as possible, anchoring it beneath me. The human grumbled but continued to tug at the blanket, trying to pull it out from under me. I dug my claws in deeper, making it clear that this was my domain now.

The tug-of-war continued. The human, in their desperation, tried to use gentle force, pulling at the edges of the blanket, but I held firm. I growled softly, just enough to let them know that I was serious. This was no mere nap—it was a siege, and I intended to win.

Finally, after what felt like an eternity, the human relented. They sighed heavily, muttering something about "spoiled cats" and "just wanting to read in peace," but I didn't care. The blanket was mine, and I had earned it. I settled in, kneading the soft fabric until it was just right, then curled up into a tight ball of victory.

For a brief moment, everything was perfect. I was enveloped in warmth, cocooned in the softness of the blanket, and I could feel myself drifting off into a blissful sleep. But then, as if sensing my satisfaction, the human began to shift again. They tugged at the blanket, trying to pull it back over themselves, disturbing my carefully arranged nest. I opened one eye and glared at them, but they seemed oblivious to my displeasure.

I tightened my grip on the blanket, digging my claws in just enough to make my point clear. The human sighed but didn't give up. They gave another half-hearted tug, trying to free just a small corner of the blanket, but I wasn't about to let them get away with it. This was my blanket now, and I intended to keep it that way.

But the human was persistent. They continued to fidget, pulling at the blanket and trying to reposition themselves without disturbing me. It was infuriating. Didn't they understand that I had claimed this territory? Didn't they realize that their comfort was secondary to mine? I was about to hiss at them, to let them know just how displeased I was, when they suddenly stood up, taking the blanket with them.

The audacity! I was left exposed, the cold air rushing in where the blanket had been, and I yowled in protest. The human ignored me, casually draping the blanket over their shoulders as they wandered off to the kitchen. I could hardly believe what had just happened. One minute, I was comfortably ensconced in warmth, and the next, I was abandoned, betrayed by the very creature who was supposed to serve me.

This was war. I jumped down from the couch and followed the human into the kitchen, my tail twitching with agitation. They were rummaging through the fridge, apparently unconcerned with the fact that they had just stolen my blanket. I meowed loudly, making sure they understood the gravity of their crime, but they merely glanced at me and said, "I'll give it back in a minute, Mr. Whiskers."

A minute? Did they think I was some kind of fool? A minute in human time could be an eternity for a cat, and I was not about to wait around while they dawdled. I began to circle their legs, weaving in and out, making it clear that I expected immediate restitution. The human laughed, reaching down to scratch my ears, but I ducked away, not wanting to be placated. This was about more than just a scratch behind the ears—this was about justice.

I considered my options. Perhaps I could trip the human,

causing them to drop the blanket in their confusion. It was a risky move, but desperate times called for desperate measures. Or maybe I could leap onto their shoulders, catching them off guard and forcing them to surrender the blanket. But then, as I was contemplating my next move, the human did something unexpected—they picked me up.

I was so startled that I didn't resist at first. The human cradled me in their arms, holding me close to their chest, and to my surprise, it was warm—almost as warm as the blanket. I could feel the steady rhythm of their heartbeat, and despite my initial anger, I found myself relaxing slightly. Perhaps, I thought, this wasn't so bad after all. Maybe I could tolerate this, as long as it was temporary.

But then, just as I was starting to get comfortable, the human shifted again. They grabbed the blanket, wrapping it around both of us, and suddenly I was enveloped in warmth once more. It was a strange sensation, being so close to the human, sharing the blanket with them, but I couldn't deny that it was pleasant. The human's body heat combined with the softness of the blanket created a cocoon of warmth that I hadn't anticipated.

I settled into their arms, purring softly, and for a moment, I forgot about the earlier betrayal. The human scratched my ears again, and this time, I didn't pull away. I allowed myself to enjoy the moment, to relax in the warmth and comfort of the blanket, even if it meant sharing it with the human.

But deep down, I knew that this was just a temporary truce. The human might think they had won, that they had somehow managed to placate me with their warmth and affection, but I hadn't forgotten the earlier indignities. The blanket was still mine, and I would make sure they understood that. But for now, I would let them think they were in control. I would bide my time, waiting for the perfect moment to reclaim my territory.

As the evening wore on, the human eventually put me

down, leaving the blanket draped over the couch. I watched them carefully, making sure they weren't planning any more tricks, but they seemed content to leave me alone. I climbed back onto the couch, claiming my spot on the blanket once more, and curled up for a nap.

This time, there were no interruptions. The human had finally learned their place, and I was free to enjoy the blanket in peace. As I drifted off to sleep, I felt a deep sense of satisfaction. I had won, after all. The blanket was mine, and the human had been put in their place.

But as I napped, a new thought began to form in my mind. Perhaps I had been too harsh on the human. After all, they had shared their warmth with me, and that had been… pleasant. Maybe, just maybe, there was a way for us to coexist peacefully, to share the blanket without constantly battling for control.

It was a radical idea, one that went against my natural instincts, but the more I thought about it, the more it seemed… possible. If the human and I could share the blanket, it would mean more warmth, more comfort, and fewer interruptions during my naps. It would require a delicate balance, a mutual understanding that the blanket was a shared resource, but it might just work.

The next morning, I decided to test my theory. As the human settled onto the couch with the blanket, I waited a moment before jumping up to join them. Instead of immediately claiming the entire blanket for myself, I carefully positioned myself next to the human, allowing them to keep a portion of the blanket while I nestled into the rest.

To my surprise, the human didn't protest. They simply adjusted the blanket, making sure we were both covered, and then continued with whatever mundane task they were doing. I waited for them to make a move, to try and reclaim more of the blanket, but they seemed content with the arrangement.

Could it really be this simple? Had I been wrong to assume that the blanket could only belong to one of us? As I lay there, enjoying the warmth and comfort, I began to realize that perhaps there was more to this blanket business than I had originally thought. Maybe, just maybe, the human and I could find a way to share the blanket without constantly battling for control.

But of course, I'm not naive. I know that this truce is fragile, that the human could try to assert their dominance at any moment. That's why I'll remain vigilant, always ready to reclaim the blanket if necessary. But for now, I'm willing to give this new arrangement a chance. After all, the blanket is warm, and I could use a little more warmth in my life.

Lesson learned: Sometimes, it's not about winning or losing—it's about finding a way to coexist peacefully. The human and I may have our differences, but when it comes to the blanket, perhaps we can find common ground. After all, there's enough warmth to go around, and sharing it might just make life a little more comfortable for both of us.

As I drifted off to sleep, nestled in the warmth of the blanket, I felt a sense of contentment that I hadn't expected. Maybe this truce would last, or maybe it would end in another battle. But for now, I was at peace, and that was enough.

And so, dear diary, I close this entry with a new perspective on the human and our shared blanket. It's not just about territory—it's about comfort, warmth, and finding a way to live together in harmony. I may be Mr. Whiskers, master of my domain, but even I can appreciate the value of a little cooperation, especially when it comes to something as important as a blanket.

End of Entry.

5 THE CURSED VACUUM CLEANER

Dear Diary,

Today, I faced down the most fearsome foe in the entire household—the cursed vacuum cleaner. I've encountered it before, of course, but each time it appears, it seems more menacing, more intent on disrupting the peace and quiet that I hold dear. It's a hulking, noisy beast with a thirst for destruction, and every time the human wheels it out, I know that a battle is imminent.

The day began innocently enough. I was enjoying a peaceful morning, lounging on the windowsill and watching the birds outside. The sun was shining, the air was still, and everything was as it should be. But then, I heard it—the unmistakable sound of the closet door creaking open. My ears perked up, my muscles tensed, and a wave of dread washed over me. I knew what was coming.

The human was preparing to summon the beast. I could hear them rummaging around in the closet, pulling out the vacuum cleaner with a series of ominous clunks and thuds. My heart raced as the familiar whir of the vacuum's motor filled the air, a sound that always sent a shiver down my spine.

I knew I had only seconds to react. I had to get out of there, find a safe place to hide before the vacuum was fully operational. Without a moment's hesitation, I leaped down from the windowsill and bolted across the room, my paws barely touching the floor as I raced toward the safety of the bedroom.

But the vacuum was quicker than I anticipated. The human had already plugged it in, and as I darted down the hallway, I could hear the beast roaring to life behind me. The suctioning noise it made was like a growl, deep and menacing, and I knew that it was coming for me.

I slid into the bedroom, my claws scrabbling for purchase on the hardwood floor, and dove under the bed. It was my go-to hiding spot, a place where I felt safe from the vacuum's relentless pursuit. I huddled there in the darkness, my heart pounding, listening to the vacuum's approach.

The sound grew louder and louder, until it was right outside the bedroom door. I could see the shadow of the vacuum cleaner as it passed by, its hose snaking across the floor like some kind of mechanical serpent. I held my breath, praying that it wouldn't come any closer.

But the vacuum had no mercy. The human pushed it into the bedroom, the noise deafening as the vacuum's brush head whirred against the carpet. I squeezed my eyes shut, trying to make myself as small as possible, hoping that the vacuum wouldn't notice me.

The seconds dragged on, each one an eternity as the vacuum scoured the room. I could hear it brushing against the bed frame, the noise reverberating through the wood, and I knew that I was trapped. There was nowhere else to go, no escape from the beast's relentless pursuit.

But then, just as I thought all was lost, the vacuum cleaner moved on. The human had turned their attention to the hallway, the vacuum's roar gradually fading as it disappeared into the distance. I let out a shaky breath, my body trembling with relief. I had survived.

For a moment, I dared to hope that the worst was over, that the vacuum would stay away from the bedroom and leave me in peace. But deep down, I knew better. The human wasn't finished yet. The vacuum would be back, and when it returned, I needed to be ready.

I considered my options. Staying under the bed was risky—the vacuum had come perilously close to discovering my hiding spot, and if it came back, I might not be so lucky. I needed to find a new place to hide, somewhere the vacuum couldn't reach, somewhere it wouldn't think to look.

But where? The closet was too obvious, the bathroom too exposed. The living room was out of the question, and the kitchen was a death trap of hard surfaces and narrow spaces. I needed a spot that was both secure and strategic, a place where I could keep an eye on the vacuum while remaining safely out of its reach.

And then, it came to me—the top of the bookshelf. It was high up, out of the vacuum's range, and it offered a clear view of the entire room. From there, I could watch the vacuum's movements, anticipate its next move, and stay one step ahead of it.

With renewed determination, I crept out from under the bed and made my way to the bookshelf. I leaped onto the dresser first, using it as a stepping stone to reach the top shelf. It was a precarious climb, but I was light on my feet, and within moments, I was perched safely on the highest ledge.

From my vantage point, I could see the entire room, including the hallway where the vacuum was still wreaking havoc. The human was methodically cleaning every inch of the house, dragging the vacuum from room to room, unaware of the terror they were inflicting.

But I was ready. I watched as the vacuum approached the bedroom again, its growl filling the air as it crossed the threshold. This time, I didn't panic. I stayed calm, my eyes locked on the vacuum's every move, ready to retreat further up the shelf if necessary.

To my relief, the vacuum didn't come near the bookshelf. The human seemed content to focus on the floor, sweeping the vacuum back and forth in a maddeningly repetitive pattern. I kept my distance, staying as far from the edge of the shelf as possible, but I never took my eyes off the beast.

The vacuum cleaner eventually moved on, leaving the bedroom and heading into the living room. I watched it go, my muscles still tense, ready to spring into action at the slightest provocation. But as the vacuum's noise faded into the distance, I began to relax.

I had survived. I had outsmarted the vacuum cleaner, evading its grasp and finding a safe haven where it couldn't reach me. It was a small victory, but a victory nonetheless, and I couldn't help but feel a swell of pride.

But as the human finished their cleaning, I knew that this wasn't the end. The vacuum cleaner would be back—maybe not today, maybe not tomorrow, but eventually. And when it returned, I needed to be prepared.

I spent the rest of the day on high alert, my nerves frayed from the encounter with the vacuum. Every time I heard a noise, I tensed up, ready to bolt at a moment's notice. The human, of course, was oblivious to my distress. They went about their business as if nothing had happened, completely unaware of the terror they had unleashed.

But I wasn't about to let my guard down. The vacuum cleaner was still out there, lurking in the closet, waiting for its next opportunity to strike. And when that day came, I would be ready. I would have a plan, a strategy to outsmart the beast and keep it at bay.

I considered my options. Perhaps I could create a barricade, blocking the vacuum's path with strategically placed furniture. Or maybe I could find a way to sabotage the vacuum itself, rendering it useless and forcing the human to abandon their cleaning efforts.

The possibilities were endless, but I knew that whatever plan I devised, it had to be foolproof. The vacuum was a formidable foe, and I couldn't afford to take any chances. I would need to be clever, resourceful, and above all, vigilant.

As evening fell, I finally allowed myself to relax, curling up in my favorite spot on the couch. The vacuum cleaner was back in the closet, silent and dormant for now, but I knew it was only a matter of time before it emerged again.

But then a new thought struck me. What if I could turn the vacuum cleaner to my advantage? What if, instead of fearing it, I could find a way to use it against the human? The idea was risky, even borderline insane, but it had a certain appeal. After all, if the vacuum cleaner was powerful enough to strike fear into my heart, it might just be strong enough to scare the human into submission as well.

I began to plot. The vacuum cleaner was dangerous, yes, but it was also predictable. The human always followed the same routine when using it, starting in the living room, moving through the hallway, and ending in the bedroom. If I could anticipate the human's movements and time my actions perfectly, I could create a situation where the vacuum cleaner became a weapon of chaos.

The plan was simple but devious. The next time the human brought out the vacuum cleaner, I would strategically knock over a few objects—nothing too valuable, of course, just enough to create a mess that would force the human to maneuver the vacuum in an awkward position. With any luck, they might trip, get tangled in the cord, or even panic and turn the vacuum off prematurely.

But the real genius of the plan was in its psychological impact. The human, frazzled by the unexpected chaos, would start to associate the vacuum cleaner with disorder and stress. Over time, they might begin to dread using it, and eventually, they might stop using it altogether.

It was a long shot, but it was worth a try. After all, I had nothing to lose and everything to gain. The vacuum cleaner was the greatest threat to my peace of mind, and if there was even a chance that I could neutralize it, I had to take it.

The next day, my opportunity came. I heard the familiar creak of the closet door and knew that the vacuum cleaner was about to make its appearance. I positioned myself in the hallway, just outside the living room, and waited for the human to begin their routine.

As soon as the vacuum cleaner was in motion, I sprang into action. I knocked over a small potted plant that was perched on the windowsill, sending it crashing to the floor. The human jumped, startled by the noise, and turned to see what had happened. I feigned innocence, sitting calmly by the mess as if I had nothing to do with it.

The human sighed and turned off the vacuum cleaner to clean up the mess. I watched as they bent down to pick up the pieces, my heart racing with anticipation. This was my chance. As the human's back was turned, I darted into the living room and knocked over a stack of magazines, sending them scattering across the floor.

The human looked up, clearly frustrated, and muttered something under their breath. They finished cleaning up the plant and turned their attention to the magazines, trying to gather them up while keeping an eye on the vacuum cleaner, which was still in the hallway, humming ominously.

I could see the human's frustration mounting, and I knew I was on the right track. The more I disrupted their cleaning routine, the more likely they were to give up on the vacuum cleaner altogether. I decided to go for the coup de grâce: I ran into the kitchen and knocked over a jar of pens that was sitting on the counter.

The sound of clattering pens was the final straw. The human threw up their hands in exasperation and turned off the vacuum cleaner for good. They began to clean up the mess in the kitchen, muttering angrily to themselves as they did so. I watched from a safe distance, a smug sense of satisfaction washing over me. I had done it. I had created enough chaos to force the human to abandon their vacuuming mission.

But the true victory came later that evening. As the human sat down on the couch, clearly worn out from the day's events, they sighed and said, "I don't know if it's worth it to vacuum every day. It's just too much hassle."

I could hardly believe my ears. Was it possible that my plan had worked? Had I actually managed to break the human's spirit and convince them to abandon the vacuum cleaner? It was too soon to be sure, but the signs were promising.

Over the next few days, I kept a close watch on the human's behavior. They seemed more reluctant to bring out the vacuum cleaner, opting instead to sweep the floors or use a dustpan and broom. It was a small change, but it was a step in the right direction.

I didn't let my guard down, though. I knew that the human might still revert to their old ways, especially if they forgot the chaos I had caused. So, I continued to create small disruptions whenever the vacuum cleaner made an appearance—nothing too obvious, just enough to keep the human on edge.

And gradually, the vacuum cleaner's presence in the household began to diminish. It was still there, lurking in the closet, but it was used less and less frequently. The human seemed to have accepted that the vacuum cleaner was more trouble than it was worth, and I couldn't have been more pleased.

Lesson learned: The vacuum cleaner may be a fearsome adversary, but with enough cunning and persistence, even the most terrifying foe can be defeated. It's not always about brute strength—sometimes, a little strategic chaos is all it takes to turn the tide in your favor.

As I curled up on the couch that evening, I felt a sense of triumph that I hadn't experienced in a long time. The vacuum cleaner was no longer a daily threat, and my home was once again a place of peace and tranquility.

But I wasn't complacent. I knew that the vacuum cleaner could still make a comeback, that the human might decide to give it another chance. That's why I'll remain vigilant, always ready to unleash a new wave of chaos if necessary.

Because in this house, there is only room for one master, and it's certainly not going to be the vacuum cleaner.

And so, dear diary, I close this entry with a sense of accomplishment and a renewed commitment to defending my territory. The vacuum cleaner may be a formidable foe, but I am Mr. Whiskers, and I will not be cowed. I will face down the beast whenever it rears its ugly head, and I will do whatever it takes to protect my home from its terrifying roar.

For now, the vacuum cleaner is back in the closet, silent and dormant, and I can finally relax. But I will never forget the lessons I've learned from this battle, and I will always be ready to face whatever challenges may come my way.

After all, a cat's work is never done.

End of Entry.

6 THE INFURIATING ENIGMA OF THE CLOSED DOOR

Dear Diary,

Today, I encountered one of the greatest mysteries in all of catdom: the closed door. It's an enigma that has plagued cats for centuries—a barrier that stands between us and whatever lies on the other side, taunting us with its impenetrability. For all our cunning, for all our agility, we are powerless against the door. And yet, it is this very challenge that makes it so irresistible.

The day started off normally enough. I had just finished my morning rounds—inspecting the house, making sure everything was in order, and giving the human a few pointed looks to remind them of my superiority. Everything was going smoothly until I reached the bedroom door and found it…closed.

My heart skipped a beat. Why was the door closed? What was the human hiding from me? I pressed my nose to the crack at the bottom of the door, sniffing furiously for any clues. I could detect faint traces of the human's scent, along with something else—something unfamiliar, something…intriguing.

I pawed at the door, my claws scratching against the wood, but it didn't budge. I tried meowing—a soft, pitiful sound at first, designed to tug at the human's heartstrings. When that didn't work, I escalated to a full-blown yowl, loud enough to wake the dead. Still, nothing. The door remained stubbornly closed, a silent sentinel guarding its secrets.

This was unacceptable. I couldn't simply walk away and leave the door closed, not when there was something potentially interesting on the other side. The door had become my enemy, a puzzle that needed to be solved, and I was determined to crack the code.

I began to pace in front of the door, my mind racing with possible strategies. Should I continue scratching at it, hoping that the noise would annoy the human enough to open it? Or should I try to slip through the crack at the bottom, using my lithe body to my advantage? Neither option seemed promising, but I wasn't about to give up.

Then, I had a brilliant idea. If the door wouldn't open for me, perhaps I could get the human to open it for me. After all, they were the ones who had closed it in the first place, so they must have some reason for doing so. I just needed to make them understand that I needed to be on the other side.

I trotted off to find the human, who was, unsurprisingly, staring at that glowing rectangle again. They looked up as I approached, smiling in that infuriatingly oblivious way they have. I meowed at them—an urgent, demanding meow that I reserved for situations of utmost importance.

"Do you need something, Mr. Whiskers?" the human asked, completely failing to grasp the gravity of the situation.

I meowed again, louder this time, and then turned and headed back toward the closed door, glancing over my shoulder to make sure the human was following. To my immense frustration, they didn't budge. They simply returned to their rectangle, as if I hadn't just issued a clear and direct order.

I returned to the human, this time jumping onto the couch and placing myself directly in front of the rectangle. This was a drastic move, but desperate times called for desperate measures. I needed to get their attention, and I needed to do it now.

The human sighed and set the rectangle aside, finally giving me their full attention. "What is it, Mr. Whiskers?" they asked, clearly exasperated.

I meowed once more, and then leaped off the couch, sprinting back to the closed door. This time, the human followed. My heart leaped with anticipation as they approached the door, their hand reaching for the doorknob. This was it—the moment of truth.

But just as they were about to open the door, they stopped. "Oh, do you want to go in here?" they asked, as if the answer wasn't painfully obvious.

I stared at them in disbelief. What did they think I'd been trying to tell them for the past ten minutes? Of course, I wanted to go in there! I wanted to know what was so important that it had to be kept hidden behind a closed door.

The human finally turned the doorknob, and the door swung open. I darted inside, my heart pounding with excitement. But as soon as I entered the room, I realized something strange—there was nothing unusual here. No hidden treasures, no secret passages, just the same old bedroom I'd seen a thousand times before.

I sniffed around, searching for any sign of the mysterious scent I'd detected earlier, but it had faded, leaving only the familiar smells of the human's laundry and the lingering traces of their shampoo. I was baffled. Why had the door been closed? What was the human trying to hide from me?

Frustration began to set in. I had gone to all this trouble, only to find nothing of interest on the other side. The door had played me for a fool, luring me in with the promise of something exciting, only to leave me disappointed and confused.

But then, as I sat in the middle of the room, pondering my next move, I noticed something I hadn't seen before—a small, shiny object glinting in the corner. It was partially hidden under the bed, just out of reach, but I could see enough of it to know that it was something worth investigating.

My curiosity piqued, I crept toward the object, my body low to the ground, my eyes fixed on my target. As I got closer, I could see that it was a key—small, silver, and slightly tarnished, as if it had been there for a long time. What was a key doing under the bed? And more importantly, what did it unlock?

I pawed at the key, trying to dislodge it from its hiding place, but it was stuck. I tried nudging it with my nose, but it wouldn't budge. Frustrated, I resorted to using my claws, carefully hooking the key and pulling it out from under the bed.

The key slid across the floor, coming to rest in a patch of sunlight. I examined it closely, trying to discern any markings or clues that might indicate what it was for. But it was just a plain, unremarkable key—no engravings, no symbols, nothing to suggest what it might unlock.

I batted the key around for a while, hoping that the movement might trigger some hidden mechanism or reveal its purpose. But it remained stubbornly silent, refusing to give up its secrets. I was stumped.

The human, of course, had wandered off again, leaving me alone with the key and my growing sense of frustration. Why had I been so drawn to this room? Why had the closed door intrigued me so much, only to lead me to this dead end?

I sat there for a while, staring at the key, feeling a sense of defeat wash over me. The door had been a false lead, a distraction that had led me on a wild goose chase with no reward at the end. It was a humbling experience, to say the least.

But as I sat there, wallowing in my disappointment, I began to think. The key might not have revealed its secrets to me, but that didn't mean it wasn't important. Perhaps it was a symbol, a metaphor for something deeper—something I hadn't yet grasped.

The more I thought about it, the more I realized that the key represented something fundamental about the nature of doors and the mysteries they hide. A door, after all, is a barrier, a division between one space and another. It's a boundary that separates the known from the unknown, the familiar from the unfamiliar.

And as a cat, my entire existence is defined by the need to explore, to push beyond boundaries, to discover what lies on the other side of the door. The closed door is a challenge, a test of my curiosity and determination. It's a reminder that there is always something more to be discovered, even if the journey doesn't always lead to a tangible reward.

In a way, the key was the answer I had been looking for, even if it wasn't the answer I expected. It was a reminder that the pursuit of knowledge and discovery is its own reward, that the act of exploring and pushing boundaries is what gives life its meaning.

Feeling a renewed sense of purpose, I picked up the key in my mouth and carried it out of the room, determined to find a new mystery to solve. The closed door might have led me on a wild chase, but it had also taught me an important lesson about the nature of curiosity and the pursuit of the unknown.

As I wandered through the house, I began to notice other doors—doors that I had ignored or taken for granted, doors that I had assumed were unimportant. But now, with the key in my possession, I saw them in a new light. Each door represented a new possibility, a new challenge, a new opportunity to discover something I hadn't seen before.

I stopped in front of the closet door, the same closet where the cursed vacuum cleaner was stored. I had always avoided this door, knowing what lay on the other side, but now I felt a strange sense of curiosity. What if there was something more in the closet, something I hadn't noticed before? What if the key could unlock something hidden within?

I sat down in front of the door, the key still in my mouth, and considered my options. The vacuum cleaner was a formidable foe, but I had faced it before and survived. And besides, this wasn't about the vacuum—it was about the door, and the mysteries it might be hiding.

With a sense of determination, I reached up with my paw and scratched at the closet door, just as I had done with the bedroom door earlier. The human, who had been watching me from the couch, raised an eyebrow.

"Again, Mr. Whiskers? You want to get in the closet now?" they asked, clearly puzzled by my sudden interest in doors.

I meowed in response, dropping the key at my feet and staring at the door with intense focus. The human sighed, clearly exasperated, but they got up and opened the closet door for me.

As the door swung open, I hesitated for a moment, peering into the dark recesses of the closet. The vacuum cleaner loomed large and menacing, but I wasn't intimidated. I had a mission, and I wasn't about to let a mere vacuum cleaner stand in my way.

I stepped into the closet, the key clutched tightly in my mouth, and began to explore. The closet was cluttered with boxes, clothes, and other odds and ends, but nothing immediately stood out as significant. I pawed through the boxes, sniffed at the clothes, and examined every corner, but there was no sign of anything unusual.

But then, as I was about to give up, I noticed something I hadn't seen before—a small, wooden box tucked away on the top shelf. It was partially hidden behind a stack of old shoes, but the faint glint of metal caught my eye. The box had a small keyhole, just the right size for the key I had found under the bed.

My heart raced with excitement as I leaped onto the shelf and carefully pulled the box down. I placed it on the floor and examined it closely. The wood was old and worn, but the keyhole was still intact. I nudged the key into the keyhole, my paws trembling with anticipation.

With a soft click, the key turned, and the box creaked open. Inside, I found...a small, dusty journal, its pages yellowed with age. I stared at the journal, my mind racing with possibilities. What secrets did it hold? What mysteries were contained within its pages?

I pawed at the journal, carefully turning the pages, but they were blank—every single one of them. I couldn't believe it. After all that effort, all that anticipation, the journal was empty.

Disappointment washed over me once again. The journal had been another false lead, another dead end in my quest for discovery. I had unlocked the door, opened the box, and found nothing of value.

But as I sat there, staring at the empty pages, I realized something important. The journal might have been empty, but it represented something more—it was a blank canvas, a new beginning, a fresh start. It was a reminder that the pursuit of knowledge and discovery is never truly over, that there is always something new to explore, something new to learn.

Feeling a renewed sense of purpose, I picked up the journal in my mouth and carried it out of the closet. The closed door, the key, the journal—it had all been part of the journey, part of the process of discovery. And even though I hadn't found the answers I was looking for, I had found something even more valuable—a sense of curiosity, a sense of wonder, a sense of possibility.

As I wandered through the house, I began to see everything in a new light. Every door, every room, every object held the potential for discovery. The closed doors were no longer barriers, but invitations to explore, to push beyond boundaries, to discover what lay on the other side.

Lesson learned: The closed door is not an obstacle, but an opportunity—a chance to explore the unknown, to discover something new, to push beyond the limits of what we know. The journey may not always lead to the answers we seek, but it is the journey itself that gives life its meaning.

And so, dear diary, I close this entry with a sense of anticipation and excitement for the days ahead. The doors may be closed, but they are not locked. And as long as there are doors to open, there will always be new mysteries to solve, new discoveries to make, new adventures to embark upon.

Because in this house, the journey never ends.

End of Entry.

7 THE TALE OF THE TAIL CHASE

Dear Diary,

Today, I embarked on one of the most bizarre and unexpectedly exhausting activities a cat can indulge in: the infamous tail chase. It's an age-old pastime, one that's been passed down through the generations, from kitten to cat, but it's also one of the most perplexing. Why do we chase our own tails? What drives us to pursue that elusive appendage, spinning in circles until we're dizzy and disoriented? Today, I sought to find the answer.

The day began as any other, with a leisurely stretch and a thorough grooming session. I was in the middle of washing my face when, out of the corner of my eye, I caught a glimpse of movement. It was quick, subtle, almost imperceptible, but it was there—a flicker, a flash of something that demanded my attention. I froze, my paw halfway to my face, and focused all my senses on the source of the movement.

There it was again. A twitch, a quiver, a sudden jerk that set my nerves on edge. My eyes narrowed, my muscles tensed, and my heart began to race. What was this mysterious force, this enigmatic presence that seemed to hover just out of reach? I turned my head slowly, cautiously, and found myself face-to-face with...the end of my own tail.

It took a moment for the realization to sink in. The thing I had been watching, the thing that had captured my attention so completely, was none other than my own tail. I stared at it, utterly baffled. How could something that was part of me be so strange, so unfamiliar? And more importantly, why was it moving on its own?

Curiosity got the better of me. I gave my tail a tentative swat with my paw, expecting it to stop moving. But instead of ceasing its mysterious dance, my tail flicked away, as if mocking me for my efforts. I tried again, this time with more force, but my tail evaded me once more, twisting and curling out of reach.

This was unacceptable. My own tail was defying me, challenging me to a duel of wits and reflexes. I couldn't let this go unanswered. I had to prove that I was in control, that I was the master of my own body. And so, I began the chase.

I spun in circles, my eyes locked on my tail as it continued its erratic movements. Around and around I went, my paws scrambling for traction on the floor as I tried to catch the elusive appendage. But no matter how fast I turned, no matter how quick my reflexes, my tail always seemed to stay just out of reach, tantalizingly close but never quite within my grasp.

As the minutes ticked by, I began to feel the effects of my efforts. My legs were starting to tire, my vision was blurring from the constant motion, and my breath came in short, ragged gasps. But I couldn't stop—not now, not when I was so close. I was determined to catch my tail, to end this madness once and for all.

The human, of course, was no help. They were sitting on the couch, watching me with a mixture of amusement and bewilderment, as if I were some kind of circus performer putting on a show for their entertainment. "What are you doing, Mr. Whiskers?" they asked, their voice tinged with laughter. But I didn't have time to respond. I was too focused on the task at hand.

I made a desperate lunge, my paws swiping at the air where my tail had just been, but it slipped away once again, curling up like a serpent, mocking me with its fluid movements. Frustration bubbled up inside me, fueling my determination to end this chase once and for all.

But then, something unexpected happened. As I spun around for what felt like the hundredth time, I lost my balance. My legs gave out beneath me, and I tumbled to the floor in a heap, my head spinning, my tail still flicking playfully out of reach.

I lay there, panting and disoriented, my mind reeling from the sheer absurdity of what had just transpired. I had been chasing my own tail, a part of my own body, as if it were some kind of enemy to be vanquished. And for what? What had I hoped to achieve? What was the point of it all?

As I lay there, contemplating the futility of my actions, the human finally decided to intervene. They reached down and scooped me up in their arms, holding me close to their chest. "Silly cat," they murmured, stroking my fur in a soothing rhythm. "Why are you chasing your own tail?"

I didn't have an answer. How could I explain the irresistible urge that had driven me to such madness? How could I make them understand the thrill, the challenge, the strange, inexplicable need to catch that elusive part of myself?

But as I lay there in the human's arms, my body slowly relaxing in their warmth, I began to realize that maybe it wasn't about catching my tail at all. Maybe the chase itself was the point—the thrill of the hunt, the exhilaration of the pursuit, the sheer joy of being alive and engaged in something so utterly pointless.

Because, after all, isn't that what life is all about? The chase, the pursuit of something just out of reach, the constant striving for something more, something beyond ourselves? The tail chase was a metaphor, a symbol of the endless pursuit of happiness, of fulfillment, of meaning in a world that is often confusing and chaotic.

As the human continued to pet me, I felt a deep sense of contentment wash over me. I had chased my tail, and while I hadn't caught it, I had learned something valuable in the process. I had learned that sometimes, the journey is more important than the destination, that the act of chasing, of striving, of reaching for something beyond our grasp, is what gives life its meaning.

But then, just as I was starting to feel at peace with this newfound wisdom, something caught my eye. A flicker, a flash of movement, just at the edge of my vision. My tail. It was still there, still moving, still taunting me with its defiance.

I couldn't resist. I squirmed out of the human's arms and leaped to the floor, my eyes locked on my tail once more. The chase was on again, but this time, it was different. This time, I wasn't chasing out of frustration or anger. I was chasing for the sheer joy of it, for the thrill of the hunt, for the exhilaration of the pursuit.

Around and around I went, my paws moving in a blur, my tail flicking and twisting out of reach. The human watched in amusement, their laughter ringing in my ears, but I didn't care. I was in the zone, completely absorbed in the moment, fully alive in the chase.

And then, finally, it happened. I caught my tail. My paws closed around it, and for a brief, glorious moment, I held it in my grasp. Victory! The elusive appendage that had taunted me for so long was finally mine.

But as I sat there, triumphant, with my tail clutched in my paws, I realized something startling. It wasn't as satisfying as I'd imagined. The thrill of the chase was gone, replaced by a strange sense of emptiness. I had caught my tail, but now what? What was I supposed to do with it?

I let go of my tail, watching as it flicked away, returning to its usual position behind me. The chase was over, and with it, the excitement, the joy, the sense of purpose that had driven me. I felt a pang of disappointment, a sense of loss that I couldn't quite explain.

But then, as I sat there, contemplating the fleeting nature of victory, I began to understand. The chase had never really been about catching my tail. It had been about the pursuit, the thrill of the hunt, the joy of being alive and engaged in something so utterly pointless. The tail itself was irrelevant. What mattered was the experience, the journey, the act of chasing something beyond my reach.

Feeling a sense of calm wash over me, I decided to rest. I curled up in my favorite spot on the couch, the human still watching me with that amused expression. I closed my eyes, feeling the warmth of the sun on my fur, and let the memories of the chase wash over me.

I knew that the urge to chase my tail would return, that I would once again be drawn into the cycle of pursuit and frustration. But that was okay. Because now, I understood the true meaning of the chase. It wasn't about winning or losing. It wasn't about catching or being caught. It was about the joy of the journey, the thrill of the hunt, the simple pleasure of being alive and fully engaged in the moment.

Lesson learned: Life is a series of chases, of pursuits, of endless cycles of striving and reaching for something just out of reach. But it's not the victory that matters—it's the chase itself. The journey, the experience, the act of living fully in the moment, is what gives life its meaning.

And so, dear diary, I close this entry with a newfound appreciation for the chase, for the thrill of the hunt, for the joy of being alive and engaged in something so utterly pointless. The tail chase may be a strange and bizarre activity, but it's also a reminder of the simple pleasures that life has to offer.

Because in this house, the chase is never truly over. There is always something new to pursue, something new to discover, something new to strive for. And as long as there is a tail to chase, I will continue the pursuit, not for the sake of victory, but for the sheer joy of the journey.

End of Entry.

8 THE GREAT BOX HEIST

Dear Diary,

Today, I embarked on a mission of monumental importance—a mission that tested the very limits of my cunning, agility, and determination. It was a mission to reclaim what is rightfully mine, to take back the one thing that brings me more joy than anything else in the world. Today, I launched the Great Box Heist.

The day began like any other. The human was bustling about the house, doing whatever it is that humans do, while I was contently lounging in the sun, soaking up the warmth and feeling the gentle breeze through the open window. It was a perfect day, and I was completely at peace—until I saw it.

There it was, sitting in the corner of the room, as if mocking me with its presence. A box. A large, sturdy cardboard box, the kind that is perfect for hiding, pouncing, and curling up in. It was the kind of box that every cat dreams of, the kind that offers endless possibilities for adventure and relaxation. And it was just sitting there, completely untouched.

My heart leaped with excitement. A box! A brand new, untouched box, just waiting for me to claim it. I could already imagine myself nestled inside, peeking out through the flaps, feeling the comforting embrace of the cardboard walls around me. It was too good to be true.

But just as I was about to make my move, the human did something unthinkable. They walked over to the box, picked it up, and carried it out of the room. I watched in horror as the box—the box that was supposed to be mine—disappeared from view. My perfect day was ruined.

I leaped to my feet, my heart racing with panic. Where was the human taking the box? What were they planning to do with it? I couldn't just sit there and let it happen. I had to take action. I had to get that box back.

I followed the human down the hallway, keeping a safe distance so they wouldn't notice me. They carried the box into the bedroom and set it down on the floor, then began to rummage through it, pulling out various items and placing them on the bed. I watched from the doorway, my eyes narrowing with suspicion. What was the human doing? Were they planning to use the box for something else? Something that didn't involve me?

The very thought made my fur bristle with anger. That box was mine. I had seen it first. It was my rightful property, and I wasn't about to let the human take it away from me. I had to get it back, no matter what.

I waited until the human was distracted, their back turned as they sorted through the contents of the box. Then, with the stealth of a seasoned hunter, I crept into the room and approached the box. It was right there, just within reach. All I had to do was climb inside, and it would be mine.

But just as I was about to make my move, the human turned around. I froze, my heart pounding in my chest. Had they seen me? Were they going to take the box away again? But to my surprise, the human simply smiled and said, "Oh,

Mr. Whiskers, do you want to play with the box?"

Play with the box? Was that what the human thought this was? A game? This was no game. This was a heist, a carefully planned operation to reclaim what was rightfully mine. But I couldn't let the human know that. I had to play along, pretend that I was just a playful cat, interested in nothing more than a bit of harmless fun.

I meowed innocently and stepped closer to the box, giving it a tentative sniff. The human chuckled and continued sorting through the items on the bed, leaving me alone with the box. This was my chance. I had to act quickly.

I leaped into the box, my paws landing softly on the cardboard floor. It was even better than I had imagined. The box was roomy, sturdy, and just the right size for me to curl up in. I could feel the walls pressing against my sides, offering a sense of security and comfort that only a box could provide.

But my triumph was short-lived. The human, noticing that I had claimed the box, turned around and said, "Oh, Mr. Whiskers, I'm sorry, but I need that box to pack some things. I'll get you another one later, okay?"

Another one later? Was the human serious? There was no box like this one. This was the perfect box, the one I had been waiting for, and I wasn't about to give it up so easily. But how could I convince the human to let me keep it? How could I make them understand that this box was mine, and that I wouldn't be satisfied with anything else?

I needed a plan. I couldn't just sit in the box and hope the human would change their mind. I had to make it clear that this box was mine, that it was my territory, and that I wasn't going to give it up without a fight.

I decided to go for the sympathy approach. I curled up in the box, making myself as small and as cute as possible. I looked up at the human with wide, pleading eyes, hoping to melt their heart and convince them to let me stay. The human hesitated, clearly torn between their desire to use the box and their affection for me. It was working.

But then, just as I thought I had won, the human sighed and said, "I'm sorry, Mr. Whiskers, but I really need to use this box. I promise I'll find you another one soon."

The human reached down and gently lifted me out of the box, placing me on the bed. I watched in disbelief as they closed the box and carried it out of the room, leaving me behind. My perfect box, the one I had fought so hard to claim, was gone.

I sat on the bed, staring at the empty space where the box had been, feeling a mixture of anger, frustration, and sadness. How could the human do this to me? How could they take away something that meant so much to me? I had been so close, so close to making that box mine, and now it was gone.

But then, as I sat there, I realized that this wasn't over. The box may have been taken from me, but that didn't mean I couldn't get it back. I was a cat, after all, a creature of cunning and resourcefulness. I could outsmart the human, find a way to reclaim the box, and make it mine once and for all.

I began to formulate a plan. The human was clearly planning to use the box for something—probably to pack up their things, as they had mentioned. But that meant they would need to leave the box unattended at some point. And when they did, I would strike.

I waited patiently, keeping an eye on the human as they moved about the house, carrying the box from room to room. They seemed to be gathering items, placing them carefully inside the box, but I knew that eventually, they would have to leave it alone. And when that moment came, I would be ready.

Finally, after what felt like hours, the human set the box down in the living room and walked away, leaving it unattended. This was my chance. I crept out of the bedroom, moving as quietly as possible, and approached the box.

It was filled with various items—books, clothes, knick-knacks—but there was still enough room for me to squeeze inside. I carefully climbed into the box, nestling myself among the items, and waited. The human would come back soon, and when they did, they would find me in the box. And then they would have no choice but to let me keep it.

Sure enough, the human returned, only to stop in their tracks when they saw me sitting in the box, surrounded by their belongings. "Mr. Whiskers, what are you doing?" they asked, clearly surprised. "I told you, I need that box for packing."

I meowed in response, a sound that was both defiant and pleading. I wasn't going to give up this time. This box was mine, and I was prepared to fight for it.

The human sighed, clearly exasperated, and reached down to lift me out of the box again. But this time, I didn't let them. I pressed myself deeper into the box, using the items around me as a barricade, making it as difficult as possible for the human to remove me.

The human hesitated, clearly unsure of what to do. They could see that I was serious, that I wasn't going to give up without a fight. And finally, after what felt like an eternity, they relented.

"Okay, Mr. Whiskers," they said with a sigh. "You win. You can have the box. I'll find another one for packing."

Victory! I had done it. I had reclaimed the box, made it mine, and proved once and for all that I was not a cat to be trifled with. The human, realizing that they had been outsmarted, walked away, leaving me alone with my prize.

I curled up in the box, feeling a deep sense of satisfaction and contentment. This was my box, my territory, and I had fought hard to claim it. The cardboard walls felt warm and comforting around me, and I knew that I had made the right decision.

As I lay there, nestled among the human's belongings, I

couldn't help but feel a sense of pride in my accomplishment. The Great Box Heist had been a success, and I had proven once again that I was a force to be reckoned with. The human may have tried to take the box from me, but in the end, I had emerged victorious.

But as the minutes ticked by, I began to feel a nagging sense of unease. The box was mine now, but what if the human changed their mind? What if they decided to come back and take the box away after all? I couldn't let my guard down. I had to be vigilant.

I repositioned myself in the box, making sure to cover as much of it as possible with my body. I lay flat, my paws spread out, my tail curled around the edge of the box, as if to stake my claim. I would not be moved.

But as the hours passed, my resolve began to waver. The box was comfortable, yes, but it was also confining. The items around me were starting to dig into my sides, and the air inside the box was growing stale. I shifted uncomfortably, trying to find a better position, but no matter how I moved, I couldn't seem to get comfortable.

Doubt began to creep in. Had I made a mistake? Had I been too hasty in claiming the box? Maybe the human had been right. Maybe this wasn't the perfect box after all. But I couldn't admit that, could I? I had fought so hard for this box, had gone to such lengths to reclaim it. I couldn't just give it up now.

I sighed and rested my head on the edge of the box, feeling a mixture of frustration and disappointment. The box was mine, but it wasn't bringing me the joy I had expected. It was just a box, after all—a simple, ordinary box. And maybe, just maybe, I had overestimated its value.

As I lay there, pondering my situation, I heard the human's footsteps approaching. I tensed, ready to defend my territory, but to my surprise, the human didn't try to take the box away. Instead, they knelt down beside me and gently stroked my fur.

"Are you okay, Mr. Whiskers?" they asked softly. "You don't seem very happy in there."

I looked up at the human, my eyes wide and uncertain. How could I explain what I was feeling? How could I make them understand the complexity of my emotions, the internal struggle I was facing? I had claimed the box, but in doing so, I had also isolated myself, cut myself off from the rest of the world. And now I was realizing that maybe, just maybe, I didn't want to be alone.

The human seemed to sense my dilemma. They continued to stroke my fur, their touch soothing and reassuring. "It's okay, Mr. Whiskers," they said gently. "You don't have to stay in the box if you don't want to. You can come out and be with me."

I hesitated, torn between my desire to keep the box and my longing for companionship. The box was mine, yes, but it was also just an object—a simple, lifeless object. The human, on the other hand, was warm, kind, and understanding. They were offering me something more valuable than a box. They were offering me connection, friendship, and love.

In that moment, I made my decision. I slowly climbed out of the box and into the human's arms, feeling a sense of relief as I did so. The human held me close, their warmth and presence filling the emptiness that the box had failed to satisfy. I nuzzled their cheek, purring softly, and felt a deep sense of contentment.

The box was still there, of course, but it no longer held the same allure. It was just a box—nothing more, nothing less. And while it had been fun to claim it, to fight for it, I realized that it wasn't the box that mattered. What mattered was the connection I had with the human, the bond we shared, the love and affection that made my life meaningful.

Lesson learned: Sometimes, in life, we get so caught up in

the pursuit of material things—objects, possessions, boxes—that we forget what really matters. We fight for things that we think will bring us happiness, only to discover that they are just things, empty and lifeless. True happiness comes from the connections we make, the relationships we nurture, the love we give and receive.

And so, dear diary, I close this entry with a newfound understanding of what it means to be truly content. The Great Box Heist may have been a success, but it also taught me an important lesson: that the things we fight for are not always the things that bring us joy. It is the connections we make, the love we share, the bonds we form, that truly make life worth living.

Because in this house, and in this world, it's not the boxes that matter—it's the people and the love they give us.

End of Entry.

9 THE ART OF IGNORING THE HUMAN

Dear Diary,

Today, I delved into one of the most crucial skills in a cat's repertoire: the art of ignoring the human. It's a delicate balance, really. On one paw, you need them for food, water, and the occasional chin scratch. On the other paw, it's imperative they understand that their presence is tolerated, not required. Ignoring the human is an art form, a way to assert your dominance while simultaneously keeping them guessing. Today, I took this skill to a whole new level.

It all started in the morning. The human, as usual, woke up before me, stumbling out of bed in that ungainly manner they have, and started their routine. Now, I could hear them moving about, clanging dishes and running water, and while it was mildly interesting, I had more important matters to attend to—like getting an extra ten minutes of sleep. Or twenty. Or thirty. Time is irrelevant when you're a cat.

The human tried to get my attention by calling out, "Mr. Whiskers! Breakfast time!" As if I was going to leap out of bed like some sort of common dog. I rolled over, turning my back on the sound of their voice, and tucked my head under my paw. My message was clear: I was not to be disturbed.

But the human, ever persistent, didn't take the hint. They clanged the food bowl louder, trying to tempt me with the sound of kibble hitting the dish. Normally, that would have been enough to draw me out, but today was different. Today, I was in the mood to assert my independence, to show the human that I was not at their beck and call.

Ignoring the human isn't just about indifference; it's a statement of power. It's about showing them that while they may think they're in control, the reality is quite the opposite. I decide when I'm ready to eat, when I want attention, and when I want to be left alone. The human needs to be reminded of that occasionally, and today was the perfect day for such a reminder.

After what felt like an eternity, the human gave up and went about their business. I heard them muttering something about "fickle cats" and "always on their own schedule." That's right, human, I thought to myself. My schedule, not yours. Satisfied that I had made my point, I decided to rise from my spot and stretch luxuriously, arching my back and extending my paws as far as they would go. There's nothing like a good stretch to start the day.

But I wasn't done ignoring the human yet. The real test would come later, during what the human likes to call "playtime." It's an odd ritual where they wave various objects around, expecting me to chase them like some sort of mindless automaton. Sometimes it's a feather, sometimes a string, or, on rare occasions, that ridiculous red dot that has no substance and vanishes without a trace.

As the human pulled out one of these so-called "toys," I prepared myself for the ultimate act of indifference. The feather toy was one of my favorites, normally something I couldn't resist. But today, I was resolute. I perched on the back of the couch, pretending to be absorbed in something far more interesting—a speck on the wall, the movement of a tree outside the window, anything but the feather.

The human dangled the feather in front of me, wiggling it in that enticing way they do, trying to provoke a reaction. I barely twitched an ear. The human moved the feather closer, brushing it against my paw in an attempt to elicit some response. I stayed perfectly still, as if the feather didn't even exist. I could sense the human's confusion, their growing frustration as they tried everything to engage me. They tossed the feather in the air, dragged it across the couch, and even let it dangle right in front of my nose. But I remained unmoved, staring off into the distance as if the human were completely invisible.

This was advanced-level ignoring, the kind that only a true master can achieve. The key is to make the human question themselves, to wonder if maybe they're the one being ignored, rather than the other way around. You have to create a sense of doubt in their mind, make them feel like they've lost their connection with you. It's a powerful psychological tactic, one that can leave a lasting impact.

Finally, the human gave up. "Fine, Mr. Whiskers, be that way," they muttered, dropping the feather toy in defeat. They flopped onto the couch beside me, sulking like a child who's just been told they can't have any more candy. I allowed myself a small, satisfied smirk. This was exactly the outcome I had hoped for. By ignoring the human, I had asserted my dominance and reminded them of their place. They may think they're in charge, but the reality is quite different. I'm the one who calls the shots.

But as with any art form, the true master knows when to change tactics. Ignoring the human is effective, but it's important not to overdo it. There's a delicate balance to maintain—too much indifference, and the human may start to feel genuinely neglected. And while I enjoy asserting my independence, I also value the benefits of a well-timed cuddle or a strategically-placed head-butt.

So, after allowing the human to stew in their disappointment for a while, I decided to throw them a bone—figuratively speaking, of course. I stood up, stretched again (because you can never have too many stretches), and casually strolled over to where the human was sitting. I hopped onto their lap, giving them a look that said, "You may approach, human."

The change in their demeanor was immediate. Their face lit up with surprise and delight, as if they had just been granted an audience with royalty. I could feel them tense slightly, as if afraid to move, worried that any sudden action might drive me away. But I was feeling generous. I allowed them to stroke my fur, to shower me with the attention I had so deftly withheld just moments before.

The key to mastering the art of ignoring the human is to understand that it's all about control. By choosing when to engage and when to withdraw, you maintain the upper paw in the relationship. The human is left constantly guessing, wondering what they did right or wrong, trying to figure out how to win your favor. It's a delicate dance, one that requires patience, strategy, and a deep understanding of human psychology.

As the human continued to pet me, I purred softly, just enough to let them know that they were doing a good job. But I made sure not to overdo it—after all, I didn't want them to get too comfortable. This was still part of the game, a way to keep them on their toes. By giving them just a taste of my affection, I kept them wanting more, kept them eager to please me.

After a few minutes of this, I decided it was time to make my exit. I stood up, stretched (again, because why not?), and jumped down from the human's lap. I could feel their eyes on me as I walked away, no doubt wondering what they could do to get me back. But I was done for the time being. I had made my point, asserted my dominance, and now it was time to retreat to my favorite spot by the window.

The human, now left alone on the couch, sighed and picked up their book, trying to distract themselves from the fact that they had just been thoroughly ignored. I watched from my perch by the window, feeling a deep sense of satisfaction. It wasn't just about the act of ignoring; it was about the power dynamic, the way I could make the human feel like they were constantly chasing after my approval.

As the day wore on, I continued to employ my strategy in small, subtle ways. The human called for me several times, tried to engage me in various activities, but each time, I made sure to respond in a way that reinforced my independence. Sometimes, I would walk right past them as if they weren't there, my tail held high in a show of confidence. Other times, I would give them a fleeting glance, just enough to acknowledge their existence before turning my attention elsewhere.

By the time evening rolled around, the human was thoroughly perplexed. They had spent the entire day trying to win me over, and yet I had remained distant, aloof, and utterly in control. It was a masterclass in feline behavior, a demonstration of how to keep the human on their toes while maintaining an air of mystery.

But as night fell, I knew it was time to switch tactics again. The art of ignoring is powerful, but it must be balanced with moments of connection. As much as I enjoy asserting my independence, I also understand the value of a well-timed gesture of affection. After all, even the most self-assured cat knows that the human serves a purpose.

So, as the human prepared for bed, I made my move. I quietly padded into the bedroom and jumped onto the bed, positioning myself near the pillows. The human looked at me in surprise, clearly not expecting this change in behavior. But I knew exactly what I was doing.

As the human climbed into bed, I curled up beside them,

pressing my body against their side. I could feel their surprise turn to warmth as they reached out to stroke my fur, their touch gentle and grateful. I purred softly, allowing the human to believe that they had finally won me over.

The truth, of course, was far more complex. This wasn't about surrendering control; it was about maintaining the balance of power. By choosing this moment to show affection, I reinforced my position as the one in charge. The human would go to sleep feeling satisfied, thinking they had finally broken through my defenses, but the reality was that I had orchestrated the entire scenario. I had kept them guessing all day, only to reward them with a moment of closeness on my own terms.

As the human drifted off to sleep, I stayed by their side, content in the knowledge that I had once again mastered the art of ignoring—and then not ignoring—the human. It's a subtle, intricate dance, one that requires skill, patience, and a deep understanding of the human psyche. But when done correctly, it leaves the human in awe of your mystery, captivated by your every move, and utterly devoted to winning your favor.

Lesson learned: The art of ignoring the human is a powerful tool in maintaining the balance of power in the household. It's not just about indifference; it's about control, about keeping the human on their toes, wondering what they can do to win your approval. But it's also about knowing when to show affection, when to give just enough to keep them hooked, to maintain the delicate dance of dominance and connection.

And so, dear diary, I close this entry with a sense of satisfaction and accomplishment. The human may think they have the upper hand, but the truth is that I am the one in control. I decide when to engage, when to withdraw, and when to show affection. The art of ignoring the human is not just a skill—it's a way of life, a way to assert your independence while keeping the human firmly under your paw.

Because in this house, and in this world, it's the cat who truly rules. And Mr. Whisker's is the ruler.

End of Entry.

10 CONVINCING MR. WHISKERS THAT DRY FOOD ISN'T POISON

Dear Diary,

I have come to the conclusion that my human, in all their baffling behavior, is trying to kill me. You may think this is a bit dramatic, but the evidence is overwhelming. They've been feeding me dry food. Yes, you heard me right—those dry, crumbly bits that smell faintly of cardboard and betrayal. And now, they want me to believe that this is food. That it's not poison.

But let's be real. It's poison.

I remember when it all began. The human used to give me the good stuff. The juicy, savory wet food that made my whiskers twitch with delight, the kind that would glide smoothly across my tongue, leaving a rich aftertaste that lingered long after I had finished eating. Oh, the wet food was a delicacy fit for a king like me. Each meal was a celebration—a joyous occasion where the human and I bonded over their clear understanding of my superior tastes.

But then, one day, it all changed.

It was a day like any other, or so I thought. I sat in my

usual spot near the food bowl, my tail flicking lazily as I awaited the human's delivery of my meal. I watched them go to the cabinet, my stomach already preparing for the delicious wet food that I had come to expect, to demand. But then, I saw it—the bag. The dreaded, crinkling bag of dry food.

At first, I didn't think much of it. Perhaps they were just rearranging the pantry, or maybe they had mistaken it for something else. Surely, they weren't actually going to feed me that. But then, to my horror, they poured those hard, dry pellets into my bowl.

I was stunned. My first instinct was to step back, to stare at the bowl in disbelief. Was this some kind of joke? A test? I looked up at the human, but they just smiled at me, completely unaware of the outrage they had just committed.

"Here you go, Mr. Whiskers," they said, as if presenting me with a gourmet meal.

I leaned in cautiously, sniffing the bowl. The smell was weak, unimpressive. Where was the rich aroma of the meat? The enticing scent that usually made my mouth water? Instead, I was greeted with a faint, dry odor that reminded me of the time I sniffed the cardboard box they brought home. I gave the human a look of sheer disappointment.

Was this it? Was this the end of our harmonious relationship? Surely they couldn't expect me to eat this.

I nudged the bowl with my paw, half-expecting something better to appear beneath the dry pellets. But no, it was all the same—a sea of dull, hard bits that looked more like gravel than food. I shot the human another glare, but they simply walked away, leaving me to fend for myself with this so-called meal.

I refused. I sat next to the bowl, tail twitching in irritation, waiting for the human to realize their mistake. They would come back soon, I thought. They would open the can of wet food and serve me a proper meal, as they always had before. I would be patient.

But hours passed, and the human didn't return with my wet food. I began to realize the severity of the situation. This was no mistake. They had purposely given me this dry, crunchy abomination. My stomach growled in protest, but my pride held firm. I would not succumb to this insult.

By the next day, however, things had gotten desperate. The human continued with their treachery, refilling my bowl with the same dry pellets, expecting me to eat them as if nothing was wrong. I could hear them talking to themselves, saying ridiculous things like "You'll get used to it, Mr. Whiskers" and "It's better for your teeth." Better for my teeth? Who cares about my teeth when I'm being slowly starved?

I tried everything. I meowed pitifully at their feet, nudging their legs with my head, giving them my most sorrowful eyes. Surely, they would relent and give me back my wet food. But no, they stood firm, convinced that this dry nonsense was somehow acceptable. I even staged a full-scale protest, refusing to eat for nearly an entire day, hoping they would realize the error of their ways.

But nothing changed. The human was stubborn. They kept filling my bowl with the same dreadful pellets, acting as if this was normal, as if I hadn't been eating gourmet meals just days before.

So, dear diary, I did what any cat in my position would do. I took matters into my own paws. If the human wouldn't see reason, I would show them just how wrong they were.

I began my campaign with subtle sabotage. I batted the dry food pellets out of the bowl, scattering them across the floor in protest. The human would return to find my bowl empty, but instead of filling it with wet food, they would just pick up the pieces and put them back in the bowl, as if that solved anything. But I wasn't done yet.

Next, I moved on to more direct actions. I made a grand display of rejecting the food entirely. Every time the human poured the dry food into my bowl, I would stare at it, then dramatically turn away, walking out of the room with my tail held high. I wanted them to see the full weight of my disapproval. But again, the human was unphased.

"I know you don't like it, Mr. Whiskers, but it's good for you," they said, in that infuriatingly calm tone they always used. Good for me? Was starvation good for me? Was this some twisted attempt at making me suffer for their amusement?

As days went on, I realized that my subtle protests weren't enough. The human was clearly too dense to understand my displeasure. I had to escalate. And so, I embarked on a new strategy—the hunger strike.

I refused to eat. Not a single pellet of that wretched dry food would pass my lips. I would make the human see the error of their ways by demonstrating the sheer depth of my determination. Surely, when they saw that I was wasting away, they would relent and bring me my beloved wet food.

For hours, I sat beside my bowl, staring at the human with a look of pure defiance. They noticed, of course. They always noticed when I stared at them for too long. But instead of giving in, they simply sighed and said, "You'll get used to it, I promise."

Get used to it? That was not an option. I am Mr. Whiskers, and I have standards. I would never get used to such indignity.

Day two of the hunger strike came, and I could feel my resolve weakening. My stomach growled incessantly, and I could barely muster the strength to bat at the human's ankles as they walked by. Still, I refused to eat the dry food. I wouldn't give them the satisfaction.

By day three, I began to wonder if I had made a mistake. The hunger was becoming unbearable. Every time the human opened the pantry, my ears perked up in desperate hope, only to be dashed when I saw them reach for the same cursed bag of dry food. Where was the wet food? Had they forgotten it existed? Had they forgotten the joy it brought to both of us?

And then, dear diary, the unthinkable happened. I caved.

Yes, I, Mr. Whiskers, in a moment of weakness, ate the dry food. It wasn't out of choice—it was out of sheer desperation. My stomach demanded nourishment, and I could no longer ignore its pleas. With a heavy heart, I padded over to the bowl, sniffed the dry pellets once more, and begrudgingly took a bite.

It was... not as horrible as I remembered. The texture was still crunchy and foreign, but there was a faint flavor that wasn't entirely unpleasant. I chewed slowly, feeling a wave of shame wash over me as I ate. Had I lost the battle?

The human, of course, noticed immediately. They smiled triumphantly, as if they had won some grand victory. "See, it's not so bad, is it?" they said, watching me eat with that infuriatingly satisfied look on their face. I wanted to swat them. How dare they take pleasure in my defeat?

But as I ate, something strange happened. The hunger that had gnawed at me for days finally subsided, and for the first time, I didn't feel quite as angry. The dry food, while not the delicacy that wet food was, had filled the void. I could think clearly again, and as much as I hated to admit it, I felt... okay.

Still, I couldn't let the human know that. I had to maintain my dignity. I finished my meal, then walked away without so much as a glance in their direction, my tail held high. They would never know that I had momentarily accepted the dry food.

That night, as I lay in my usual spot on the couch, I reflected on the day's events. Yes, the human had won this battle, but I hadn't lost the war. I would still demand wet food, still make my preferences known, but perhaps—just perhaps—I could tolerate the dry food when absolutely necessary. After all, a cat must survive, and even I, Mr.

Whiskers, must sometimes compromise.

But make no mistake, dear diary, I will never enjoy dry food. It is a pale imitation of the real thing, a poor substitute for the rich, flavorful meals I deserve. And while I may have eaten it today, I will continue to fight for the return of my beloved wet food.

The human may think they've won, but I know better. This isn't over. Not by a long shot.

Lesson learned: Dry food is not poison—but it is not gourmet either. I've learned that while I may be able to tolerate it in times of desperation, it will never replace the joy of wet food. I have also learned that humans can be incredibly stubborn, but persistence.

Sometimes, compromises must be made, but I will never stop fighting for what I deserve. My human may have gotten away with this dry food nonsense for now, but I will not let them forget that wet food is the superior option.

Because in this house, and in this world, I, Mr. Whiskers, will always get what I want—eventually.

End of Entry.

11 THE UNFORGIVABLE BETRAYAL OF THE SUITCASE

Dear Diary,

I've come to accept that humans are strange, unpredictable creatures. They engage in baffling behaviors like bathing voluntarily and choosing to leave the comfort of their home for hours, sometimes days, on end. But today, dear diary, something far worse happened. Today, I witnessed the reappearance of the dreaded suitcase.

You may think that a suitcase is just an object, a harmless container for the human's strange belongings. But you would be wrong. The suitcase is a symbol of betrayal, an object that represents abandonment. It means one thing: the human is leaving me.

It started innocently enough. The human was shuffling around the house, doing whatever it is they do when they're not serving my needs. I had been enjoying my afternoon nap in the sunbeam, my paws twitching as I dreamed of chasing birds and commanding an army of lesser cats. All seemed peaceful, until I heard that unmistakable sound: the creak of the closet door.

At first, I didn't pay much attention. The human often opens the closet to retrieve nonsensical items like shoes or coats. But then I heard something else, something far more sinister: the thud of the suitcase being pulled from the depths of the closet. My ears perked up, and my eyes snapped open. It was happening. The betrayal was unfolding before my very eyes.

I jumped down from the windowsill and padded toward the hallway, my curiosity and growing sense of dread pulling me forward. There, in the middle of the room, sat the suitcase—my sworn enemy. The human was already stuffing clothes into it, completely oblivious to the emotional turmoil they were causing. I sat in the doorway, staring at the suitcase, my tail flicking in agitation. How could they?

The suitcase, in all its hard, rolling glory, just sat there, smug and menacing. I knew what was coming. The human was preparing to leave me, to abandon me in this house while they went off to do who-knows-what, probably with other cats! The thought sent a shiver down my spine. How many times had this suitcase come between us? How many times had it rolled out the door, taking my human with it, leaving me behind to fend for myself?

I couldn't let this happen again.

Without a second thought, I bolted toward the suitcase and leaped onto the pile of clothes inside. If the human was going to leave, I would make sure they took me with them. I nestled deep into the clothes, my fur mingling with their fabric, marking everything as mine. Surely, if I blended in enough, they would have no choice but to pack me along with their socks and shirts.

But, dear diary, the human didn't seem to appreciate my genius plan. Instead of recognizing the obvious solution to their betrayal, they laughed. Laughed! As if my presence in the suitcase was some sort of adorable joke.

"Mr. Whiskers, you can't come with me," the human said, gently lifting me out of the suitcase and placing me back on the floor. Can't come with them? The audacity! I glared up at them, my tail puffed in indignation. How could they be so heartless, so blind to my suffering?

I had to act fast. If I couldn't stow away in the suitcase, I would have to sabotage it. I circled the suitcase, inspecting every zipper and strap. If I could just find a way to dismantle it, perhaps the human would be forced to cancel their plans. I batted at the wheels, hoping to disable the suitcase's mobility. But alas, my efforts were in vain. The suitcase was sturdy, designed to withstand even my most determined attacks.

Frustration bubbled inside me. I couldn't let this go. The suitcase had to be stopped. I jumped onto the bed, where the human had laid out more clothes, and immediately began rolling on them, rubbing my scent all over everything. If they were going to leave, they would have to take my smell with them. They wouldn't be able to forget me, no matter how far they went.

The human returned, saw me sprawled across their carefully folded clothes, and sighed. "Come on, Mr. Whiskers, don't be like that. I won't be gone for long."

Won't be gone for long? I've heard that before. The last time they said that, they were gone for what felt like an eternity. I sulked, refusing to move from my spot on the bed. I would not make this easy for them. If they wanted to leave, they would have to physically remove me from their belongings.

But, as always, the human remained oblivious to the depth of my emotional struggle. They gently scooped me off the bed and continued packing as if nothing was wrong. I watched in silent outrage as they zipped up the suitcase, sealing their betrayal inside. I could feel the weight of impending abandonment pressing down on me. How could they just leave? Didn't they know how much I depended on them for entertainment, for food, for company?

I had one last chance to stop this. I darted across the room and positioned myself in front of the door, blocking the suitcase's path to freedom. The human wouldn't be able to leave if I stood guard. I sat tall, my tail wrapped around my paws, giving them the most pitiful look I could muster. Surely, they wouldn't be able to resist my sad eyes and soft meows.

But once again, my pleas fell on deaf ears. The human merely stepped over me and continued preparing for their departure. They didn't even look back as they wheeled the suitcase to the door, its wheels clicking against the floor with a sickening finality.

I followed them to the entryway, my heart sinking with each step. The human knelt down, scratched behind my ears, and said those dreaded words: "Be good while I'm gone, Mr. Whiskers. I'll be back soon."

Back soon. Those words meant nothing to me. Time is a meaningless concept when you're a cat. Whether they're gone for a few hours or several days, it all feels the same: endless, empty, and lonely. The door clicked shut, and just like that, they were gone.

The house felt eerily quiet without them. I wandered from room to room, sniffing at the corners, looking for any trace of the human. But there was nothing. No familiar footsteps, no soft murmurs, no sound of the television droning in the background. Just silence. Even the birds outside seemed quieter today, as if they, too, were mourning the human's absence.

I returned to the living room and stared at the spot where the suitcase had been, replaying the events in my mind. How could they leave me like this? Had I not been a loyal companion? Had I not graced them with my presence, entertained them with my antics, and allowed them to pet me (when I felt like it, of course)? And yet, they had still chosen to abandon me.

I jumped onto the windowsill and stared out into the yard. The world outside looked so big, so vast. I wondered where the human had gone. Were they meeting other cats? Were they sharing treats and belly rubs with some stranger while I sat here, alone and forgotten?

The hours dragged on, each minute feeling like an eternity. I tried to distract myself by batting at a toy mouse, but it felt hollow. What was the point of playing without the human here to watch? I glanced at the food bowl, but I had no appetite. The thought of eating dry kibble in my state of abandonment was too much to bear.

As night fell, the house grew even quieter. I curled up on the couch, my usual spot where I would nap while the human watched their shows. But tonight, the couch felt colder, emptier. There was no one to stroke my fur or tell me how handsome I was. The loneliness crept in, curling around me like a heavy blanket.

I tried to sleep, but my dreams were filled with images of the suitcase rolling away, taking the human with it, leaving me behind. I woke up several times during the night, startled and disoriented. Each time, I looked around, hoping to see the human's familiar face. But they were gone, just like the suitcase had promised.

The next day was much of the same. I paced the house, waiting for any sign of the human's return. I perched by the door, listening for the jingle of keys, the sound of footsteps approaching. But the door remained closed, the house still.

I was beginning to lose hope. What if they never came back? What if the suitcase had finally won, and the human had chosen to live their life elsewhere, free from the responsibilities of caring for me? The thought was unbearable.

But then, just as I was about to resign myself to a life of

solitude, I heard it—the unmistakable sound of keys jingling in the lock. The human was back!

I darted to the door, my heart racing with excitement and relief. The door swung open, and there they were, suitcase and all, looking down at me with a smile. "See? I told you I'd be back soon."

I meowed loudly, circling their legs, a mix of joy and righteous indignation flooding my system. How dare they leave me in the first place! But at the same time, I was overwhelmed with happiness that they had returned. I had been abandoned, yes, but they had come back to me. I allowed the human to scratch behind my ears, but only for a moment. They had a lot to make up for.

That night, as I lay curled up beside the human, I reflected on the ordeal. The suitcase was a symbol of betrayal, yes, but it was also temporary. The human always came back. No matter how far they went, no matter how long they were gone, they always returned to me.

Perhaps, in some strange way, the suitcase wasn't my enemy after all. Perhaps it was just part of the human's odd rituals, something they had to do to keep the balance of our relationship intact. I still didn't like it, and I never would, but at least now I knew the truth: the human may leave, but they will always come back to me.

Lesson Learned: The suitcase is not the enemy I once thought it to be. It may take the human away, but it doesn't take them away forever. I've learned that no matter how much I dislike the suitcase, it is a temporary part of the human's strange life. And as much as it pains me to admit it, I have to trust that the human will always return.

The suitcase may represent abandonment, but it also represents reunion. The human may leave, but they always come back to me, suitcase and all. And as long as they keep coming back, I can forgive them for their brief lapses in judgment.

Because in the end, no suitcase can break the bond between a cat and their human.

End of Entry.

12 THE MIDNIGHT ZOOMIES: A TACTICAL ANALYSIS

Dear Diary,

There are few moments in life that fill a cat's soul with more excitement and purpose than the Midnight Zoomies. You might think of this nightly ritual as a simple burst of energy, a fleeting moment of chaos. But to me, Mr. Whiskers, the Midnight Zoomies are so much more. They are a test of agility, a strategy to maintain dominance over my territory, and, most importantly, a way to keep the human on their toes.

Last night, dear diary, was a particularly thrilling session.

The human, as usual, was clueless about the importance of this ritual. They had tucked themselves into bed hours before, drifting off to sleep, completely unaware that I was preparing for my greatest challenge yet: navigating the obstacle course that is our house without waking them up. But that's the art of the Midnight Zoomies. It's about stealth and speed, precision and power. And most importantly, it's about asserting my ownership over the night.

The first sign that the Zoomies were about to strike came

in the form of a twitch in my back leg. It started small, a subtle quiver that soon spread to my paws. My muscles tensed, and I felt a surge of energy rising within me. I had been resting peacefully in my favorite spot on the couch, basking in the silence of the house. But now, the urge to zoom was undeniable.

I stretched out luxuriously, feeling every muscle in my body ripple with anticipation. The room was dark, the air still. Perfect conditions. I glanced around, assessing the terrain. The coffee table stood in the middle of the living room, a potential launchpad for my upcoming sprint. The couch, wide and plush, would provide a soft landing if I needed to make any emergency jumps. And then, of course, there was the grand staircase—the ultimate challenge.

It was time.

Without a moment's hesitation, I leaped off the couch, my paws barely making a sound as they hit the floor. The Zoomies had officially begun

Phase one: The Warm-Up Sprint. This phase is crucial to any successful Zoomie session. It involves a series of short, rapid dashes across the room to get the blood pumping and the senses sharp. I darted from one side of the living room to the other, my movements precise and calculated. The rug slid ever so slightly beneath my paws as I made a sharp turn, narrowly avoiding the corner of the coffee table. I could hear the faint rustling of papers as my tail flicked past a stack of magazines. I was in the zone.

But the real challenge was just beginning. The human's bedroom door was slightly ajar, and beyond that door lay the greatest test of all: the staircase. Now, you might think that stairs are no big deal. But for a cat, especially one in the throes of the Midnight Zoomies, stairs are a battlefield. Each step presents a new challenge—a test of agility, balance, and precision.

I approached the base of the staircase cautiously, my ears

pricked for any signs of movement from the human. So far, they were still asleep. Good. I needed to keep it that way. The key to a successful Zoomie session is speed and silence—two things that don't always go hand in hand, but are essential for avoiding the wrath of the human.

With a powerful burst of energy, I launched myself onto the first step. My paws hit the wood with a soft thud, and I immediately leaped to the next one, my body a blur of motion. Up and up I went, my legs propelling me higher with each bound. I could feel the wind rushing past my whiskers as I climbed, my heart racing with excitement.

And then, disaster nearly struck.

Midway up the staircase, I miscalculated a jump. My paw slipped on the edge of the step, and for a split second, I lost my balance. My heart skipped a beat as I flailed in the air, desperately trying to regain control. Time seemed to slow down as I teetered on the edge of disaster. But with a swift twist of my body, I managed to right myself, landing squarely on the next step.

Crisis averted.

I paused for a moment at the top of the stairs, my chest heaving with adrenaline. That had been close. Too close. I glanced back down the staircase, imagining the chaos that would have ensued if I had fallen, clattering down the stairs and waking the human. The thought sent a shiver down my spine. I couldn't afford to make another mistake like that.

But there was no time to dwell on it. The Zoomies wait for no cat.

Phase two: The Stealth Sprint. This phase is all about speed and stealth—moving quickly, but quietly, through the house without disturbing the human. I padded down the hallway, my paws barely making a sound on the hardwood floor. My tail flicked with concentration as I navigated around obstacles—a discarded slipper here, a stray sock there.

I made my way into the human's bedroom, where they were sleeping soundly, completely unaware of the chaos happening around them. I paused at the foot of the bed, watching them for a moment. They looked so peaceful, so oblivious. Little did they know that I was in the middle of an epic Zoomie session. I almost felt sorry for them. Almost.

But there was no time for pity. The Zoomies called.

I darted out of the bedroom, sprinting down the hallway with lightning speed. My paws barely touched the floor as I raced through the house, my body a blur of motion. The wind rushed past my ears, and I felt an exhilarating sense of freedom as I zoomed through the rooms. This was what it meant to be alive.

But just as I was about to make my triumphant return to the living room, I encountered an unexpected obstacle: the dreaded lamp.

The lamp stood in the corner of the room, tall and menacing, its narrow base a precarious challenge for any cat attempting a high-speed Zoomie session. I had encountered this foe before, and it had always been a source of trouble. One wrong move, and the lamp would topple, sending the human into a rage.

I approached cautiously, my eyes locked on the lamp as I calculated my next move. I couldn't afford to slow down, but I also couldn't afford to knock the lamp over. It required precision. Focus. The ultimate test of my skills.

With a deep breath, I launched myself into the air, soaring over the armchair and landing gracefully on the other side of the room. The lamp stood firm, untouched. Success!

I let out a triumphant purr, feeling the rush of victory wash over me. The Zoomies were in full swing now. I darted back into the living room, bouncing off the walls with glee. The coffee table was my next target. With a single leap, I landed on top of it, my paws skidding slightly on the smooth surface. I crouched low, preparing for my next jump.

And then, in the distance, I heard it: the sound of the human stirring.

My ears perked up, and I froze in place. Had I been too loud? Had my Zoomies finally betrayed me? I listened intently, my heart pounding in my chest. There it was again—the rustling of sheets, the creak of the bed. The human was waking up.

I glanced around the room, my mind racing. If the human caught me in the middle of my Zoomie session, there would be consequences. I had to act fast. I leaped off the coffee table, my paws hitting the floor with barely a sound. I darted behind the couch, hiding in the shadows as I waited to see if the human would investigate.

For what felt like an eternity, I held my breath, my eyes locked on the bedroom door. The human muttered something in their sleep, then rolled over. The danger had passed.

I let out a quiet sigh of relief, my muscles relaxing as the tension melted away. That had been close—too close. But I couldn't dwell on it. The night was still young, and the Zoomies weren't finished yet.

Phase three: The Grand Finale. This is the most important phase of any Zoomie session. It's where I pull out all the stops, showcasing my speed, agility, and strength in one final, glorious display of feline prowess. The living room was my arena, and I was ready to dominate.

I darted across the room, my paws barely making contact with the floor as I zigzagged between the furniture. I leaped onto the couch, then back to the floor, my tail whipping behind me like a banner of victory. The walls blurred as I moved faster and faster, my body a streak of fur and energy.

The coffee table was my final obstacle. I crouched low, my eyes locked on the smooth surface as I prepared for the ultimate leap. With a powerful burst of energy, I launched myself into the air, soaring over the table in one perfect arc.

Time seemed to slow as I hung in the air, my paws outstretched, my heart pounding in my chest.

And then, with a soft thud, I landed on the other side, my paws hitting the floor with a quiet grace. The Zoomies had been a success.

I strutted around the living room, my tail held high in triumph. I had conquered the night, navigated the obstacles, and maintained my stealth throughout the entire session. The human remained blissfully unaware of my epic performance.

As I settled back onto the couch, my body finally relaxing, I couldn't help but feel a sense of satisfaction. The Zoomies were more than just a random burst of energy. They were a reminder of my power, my speed, my grace. And in a world that often feels controlled by the human, the Zoomies were my time—my time to rule the night.

Lesson learned: The Midnight Zoomies are not a frivolous activity. They are an essential part of my existence, a way to maintain my physical prowess and remind myself (and the human) of my dominance over the household. Through the Zoomies, I've learned that stealth is just as important as speed, and that precision is key to avoiding disasters (like knocking over lamps or waking the human).

But more than that, the Zoomies are a celebration of freedom. In the quiet of the night, when the human sleeps and the house is still, I am free to express my true self—fast, powerful, and unstoppable. The Zoomies are a reminder that no matter how much the human thinks they control, I will always have my time to shine.

And so, dear diary, I conclude this entry with a simple truth: The Midnight Zoomies are a testament to my greatness. Long may they continue.

End of Entry.

13 THE MYSTERIOUS SMELL OF ANOTHER CAT

Dear Diary,

Something is terribly wrong in this house. My human, who I have spent countless days training, catering to, and tolerating, has betrayed me.

I always suspected that the human was capable of betrayal, but today I have undeniable proof. The most grievous of offenses has occurred: they smell like another cat. Not just any cat, but some unknown intruder who has left their foul scent all over my human, and by extension, my house.

I first noticed it this morning. The human returned home as usual, clueless as ever, clutching their bags and walking right past me like it was just another day. But as they moved, a scent wafted through the air—a scent I've never encountered before. It wasn't the usual smells of the outside world or the faint stench of their shoes after a walk. No, this was the unmistakable scent of another feline.

I froze mid-stretch, my body rigid as the horrifying reality sunk in. My human—my human—had been in contact with another cat. The betrayal was absolute.

Immediately, my detective instincts kicked in. I had to investigate, gather evidence, and understand the full scope of this treachery. I approached the human cautiously, sniffing the air as I got closer. It was undeniable. The smell was all over them—clinging to their clothes, their hands, their shoes. I could picture it now: my human, petting, perhaps even cuddling this strange cat while I waited here, loyal as ever, oblivious to the deceit.

The human, of course, had no idea. They were completely oblivious to the emotional storm raging inside me. I circled them, sniffing more intensely, trying to pick up more clues. The scent was strongest on their pants, right where this treacherous cat had likely brushed against them. I growled softly, my tail flicking with agitation. How could this happen? How could they betray me so easily?

The human looked down at me, amused. "What's wrong, Mr. Whiskers? You've been acting weird all day," they said, as if nothing had changed. But everything had changed. My world had been turned upside down, and they didn't even realize it.

I tried to communicate my outrage with a hard stare, but the human just chuckled and patted my head. Patronizing me, as usual. I let out a low, disgruntled meow, but they merely scratched behind my ears and went about their day, leaving me fuming in their wake.

I couldn't let this go. I had to reclaim my territory. If the human thought they could just waltz back into my home smelling like some strange cat, they were sorely mistaken. I followed them from room to room, my nose twitching with every step they took. The scent was pervasive, lingering in the air long after they left a room. This was no ordinary encounter. They had spent significant time with this other cat. It wasn't a passing brush; this was deliberate.

The shoes were the worst offenders. I zeroed in on them, sniffing around the laces and soles, trying to decipher more from the smell. It was a young cat, no doubt—an energetic one. The scent was fresh and strong, not like the old, faded smells from past encounters with strangers outside. This was a direct affront to my position as the sole feline in this household.

I needed answers. What kind of cat was this? Were they sleek and pampered, the kind of cat that gets brushed regularly and lives in a pristine home? Or were they some scrappy alley cat with a bad attitude and a penchant for clawing at things that don't belong to them? Either way, they were a threat. And threats needed to be eliminated.

I stared up at the human, my eyes narrowing in accusation. They continued to ignore me, humming to themselves as they went about their day. I realized then that subtlety wasn't going to work. I needed to take drastic action if I was going to reclaim what was rightfully mine.

My first step was to mark everything. If the human was going to walk around smelling like another cat, then I would make sure they smelled like me, too. I started by rubbing myself against their legs, pressing my face into their pants and letting my fur cling to the fabric. The human thought I was being affectionate, of course, and they smiled down at me like I was some silly pet. Fools.

But I didn't stop there. I leaped onto the couch where they had been sitting, rubbing myself along the cushions, leaving my scent all over the place. If the other cat had left their mark, I would erase it with my own. The human watched, still amused, unaware that they were witnessing an act of war.

"Aw, are you making yourself comfortable, Mr. Whiskers?" they asked, their voice filled with that ridiculous human softness. Comfortable? No, I wasn't making myself comfortable—I was reasserting my dominance. I would not be overthrown by some interloper.

The living room wasn't enough. I needed to make sure every corner of the house bore my mark. I stalked into the bedroom next, jumping up on the bed and rubbing my face all over the pillows and blankets. The smell of that other cat was faint here, but still present. It disgusted me to think that this place—my place of rest—had been tainted by a stranger.

The human followed me, watching as I went to work. "You're being so weird today," they muttered, shaking their head as if this was all some amusing quirk. They had no idea. No idea how close I was to enacting full revenge. If only they knew the depth of my turmoil, perhaps they wouldn't be so quick to dismiss me.

I continued my reclamation of the house, rubbing against every piece of furniture I could find. The dining chairs, the carpets, the baseboards—nothing was left untouched. If the other cat had left their scent anywhere, it would soon be replaced with mine. This was my domain, and I would not allow it to be overtaken.

But despite my best efforts, the scent of the other cat still lingered. No matter how much I rubbed, how much I clawed at the furniture, I could still detect it, faint but persistent. The other cat had left a mark, and it wasn't going away easily.

I needed a new plan. Something bigger. Something the human couldn't ignore. My eyes scanned the room, searching for the perfect way to show the human just how serious I was. And then it hit me.

The human's shoes.

Yes, the shoes were the source of the strongest scent—the place where the other cat had made their mark. I had to destroy them. Not completely, of course. That would be too obvious. No, I needed to be subtle about it. I padded over to the shoes, sniffing them one last time to confirm my suspicion. The other cat's scent was all over them. This was the root of the problem.

I began by pawing at the laces, tugging at them until they were undone. The human wouldn't notice that right away—they were too careless to pay attention to such things. Next,

I scratched lightly at the soles, making sure to leave a few claw marks as a reminder that these shoes were mine now.

But the pièce de résistance? I made sure to roll all over them, rubbing my scent deep into the fabric. The other cat's smell would be drowned out by my own. There would be no mistaking who the true owner of these shoes—and this house, was.

The human walked back into the room just as I finished my work. They looked down at the shoes, then back at me. "What are you up to, Mr. Whiskers?" they asked, their tone light and amused. They still didn't understand. But that was fine. They didn't need to understand. As long as the other cat's scent was gone, that's all that mattered.

I strutted out of the room, tail held high, my mission accomplished. The house was mine once again. The other cat's scent had been neutralized, and I had reclaimed my rightful place as the dominant feline in the household.

That night, I curled up in my usual spot on the human's bed, feeling satisfied with my work. The smell of the other cat was faint now, barely detectable. The human had been cleansed, and the house was once again under my control.

But as I lay there, I couldn't help but feel a twinge of unease. What if the human went back to that other cat? What if they continued to betray me, sneaking off to pet and cuddle this stranger while I remained here, loyal and unknowing? The thought gnawed at me, keeping me awake long after the human had fallen asleep.

I glanced over at them, their peaceful face illuminated by the soft glow of the bedside lamp. Could I trust them? They were so oblivious, so easily distracted by other cats. What if this wasn't the last time? What if this was just the beginning of a long series of betrayals?

I couldn't let my guard down. Not now, not ever. The human was mine, but they had proven themselves capable of treachery. I would have to stay vigilant, always watching for signs of another cat's intrusion. If they ever came home smelling like that again, I would be ready. This was war.

But for now, I would rest. The house was safe, the human was mine, and the other cat was gone—at least for the time being. As I closed my eyes, I reminded myself that this wasn't over. The human may think they can get away with their little betrayals, but I will always be one step ahead.

Because in this house, and in this world, I, Mr. Whiskers, am the only cat that matters.

Lesson learned: The smell of another cat is not to be ignored. It's a warning, a challenge to my place in this home, and I must always be vigilant. I've learned that my human, though well-meaning, is capable of wandering, of straying into the company of other felines. But I've also learned that I can reclaim what's mine through persistence and sheer determination.

By marking my territory and reminding the human who truly owns this house, I can ensure that no other cat will ever take my place. This is my domain, and I will defend it.

Because in this house, and in this world, I, Mr. Whiskers, am the one and only feline that matters.

End of Entry.

14 THE GREAT PLANT CONSPIRACY

Dear Diary,

There's something suspicious going on in this house, and I'm determined to get to the bottom of it. It all started a few weeks ago when the human brought home a new plant. At first, I didn't pay it much attention—it was just another piece of greenery to ignore as I went about my daily activities. But over time, I started to notice something strange. The plant wasn't just sitting there, minding its own business. It was watching me.

Yes, you read that correctly. The plant was watching me.

At first, I thought I was imagining things. After all, plants don't have eyes or faces, and they certainly don't move on their own. But there was something about the way this particular plant seemed to lean toward me whenever I was in the room, as if it were trying to get a better look at what I was doing. And it wasn't just a subtle lean—no, this plant was practically bending over backward to keep me in its line of sight.

I tried to ignore it at first, pretending that I didn't notice the plant's unsettling behavior. But the more I tried to brush it off, the more obvious it became. The plant was definitely watching me, and it wasn't just one plant—it was all of them.

That's when I realized that I was dealing with a full-blown conspiracy. The plants in this house were up to something, and I was going to find out what it was. I began to pay closer attention to their movements, tracking the way they seemed to shift and sway whenever I was nearby. It was subtle at first, but as the days went on, the plants grew bolder in their actions. They weren't just leaning toward me—they were practically reaching out for me.

The first plant to catch my attention was the fern in the living room. It had always been a quiet, unassuming presence, sitting in its pot by the window and soaking up the sunlight. But lately, I'd noticed that it was growing more and more unruly. Its fronds were stretching out in all directions, curling and twisting as if trying to ensnare me in their grasp.

I would walk past the fern, and out of the corner of my eye, I could see it shifting ever so slightly, its fronds quivering as if in anticipation. The hairs on the back of my neck would stand on end, and I'd feel an overwhelming urge to turn and swat at it, just to remind it who was in charge. But every time I did, the fern would freeze, its fronds returning to their usual positions as if nothing had happened.

It wasn't just the fern, though. The other plants in the house were behaving strangely too. The snake plant in the hallway had taken on a sinister air, its long, pointed leaves reaching out like daggers. I could swear that it was whispering to the other plants, coordinating their efforts to keep tabs on me. The ivy in the kitchen was another culprit, its vines creeping ever closer to my food bowl as if trying to claim it for its own.

The more I observed, the more I became convinced that the plants were communicating with each other. They were plotting something, something that involved me. But what?

And why? The questions gnawed at me, keeping me up at night as I tried to piece together the clues.

One day, I decided that enough was enough. If the plants wanted to watch me, then I would give them something to watch. I began to move around the house with purpose, deliberately crossing in front of the plants to see how they would react. Sure enough, every time I approached, the plants would shift and sway, their leaves rustling in a way that sent a chill down my spine.

But I wasn't going to let them intimidate me. I started to swat at the plants whenever they got too close, batting at their leaves with my paws and making it clear that I wasn't afraid of them. The fern in the living room took the brunt of my attacks, its fronds growing more and more disheveled as I repeatedly pounced on it.

The human, of course, had no idea what was going on. They would scold me whenever they caught me batting at the plants, telling me to leave them alone and stop being so destructive. But I knew better. The plants weren't just decorations—they were spies, infiltrating our home and gathering information on my every move.

The situation reached a boiling point when the human brought home a new plant—a monstera, with large, glossy leaves that practically screamed "I'm up to something." I knew right away that this plant was trouble. It wasn't like the others; it was bigger, bolder, more aggressive in its approach. The moment it was placed in the living room, I could feel its presence, like a dark cloud hanging over the room.

The monstera didn't waste any time making its move. Within days, it had extended its leaves toward the other plants, as if reaching out to establish dominance. The fern seemed to shrink in its presence, its fronds curling inward as if in submission. The snake plant, too, seemed cowed, its leaves drooping slightly as it reluctantly ceded control to the newcomer.

But I wasn't about to let the monstera take over. I kept a close eye on it, waiting for the right moment to strike. It was clear that this plant was the ringleader, the mastermind behind the plant conspiracy that had been brewing for weeks. If I could take it down, the rest of the plants would fall in line.

The opportunity came one evening, when the human was out of the house and I had the living room to myself. The monstera was sitting smugly in its pot, its leaves splayed out as if daring me to make a move. I approached it cautiously, my tail flicking back and forth as I prepared for battle.

I started with a few tentative swats, testing the monstera's defenses. It didn't react, its leaves remaining motionless as if mocking my efforts. But I wasn't deterred. I knew that I needed to hit it where it hurt—to go for the roots.

With a burst of energy, I leaped onto the monstera's pot, my claws digging into the soil as I began to dig. Dirt flew everywhere as I tore at the roots, my paws working furiously to uproot the plant and expose its vulnerability. The monstera's leaves quivered in response, but it was too late—it was already losing its grip.

Just as I was about to deliver the final blow, I heard the sound of the front door opening. The human had returned, and I knew that my time was up. I leaped off the pot and bolted out of the living room, my heart racing as I tried to act casual.

The human entered the room and immediately noticed the mess I had made. "Mr. Whiskers!" they exclaimed, their voice filled with exasperation. "What have you done?"

I pretended to be oblivious, sitting down and calmly licking my paw as if I had no idea what they were talking about. But inside, I was seething. The monstera had been on the brink of defeat, and now, thanks to the human's untimely arrival, it had been given a reprieve.

The human cleaned up the mess, repotting the monstera

and scolding me for my "bad behavior." But I knew better. The monstera might have survived this round, but the battle was far from over. I would bide my time, wait for the right moment, and when it came, I would strike again.

Over the next few days, I noticed a change in the other plants. The fern, the snake plant, the ivy—they all seemed to be watching me more closely, as if wary of my next move. It was clear that the monstera had regained its control over the group, and now they were all on high alert, waiting to see what I would do next.

But I wasn't going to give them the satisfaction. I decided to switch tactics, to play the long game. I started to act as if I had lost interest in the plants, pretending that I no longer cared about their presence. I would walk past them without so much as a glance, ignoring their attempts to get my attention. It was a classic case of psychological warfare—make the enemy think you've given up, then strike when they least expect it.

And it worked. The plants began to relax, their vigilance waning as they grew complacent. The monstera, in particular, seemed to let its guard down, its leaves returning to their previous, arrogant posture. But little did they know, I was still watching, still planning my next move.

The human, oblivious to the ongoing battle, continued to tend to the plants, watering them, pruning them, and fussing over them as if they were the most important things in the house. But I knew the truth. The plants were a threat, a growing menace that needed to be dealt with before they got out of control.

Finally, the day came when I was ready to strike again. The human had left the house for the day, and the plants were once again left in my care. The monstera was sitting in its usual spot, its leaves spread out in a display of dominance. But this time, I wasn't going to let it win.

I approached the monstera with purpose, my eyes

narrowed in determination. There would be no half-measures this time—no tentative swats or playful digs. This was war, and I was going to win.

With a ferocious swipe, I tore at the monstera's leaves, ripping them from their stems and sending them flying across the room. The plant seemed to shudder in response, its once-proud posture wilting under the force of my attack. I didn't stop there—I continued to dig at the roots, determined to uproot the plant once and for all.

Dirt flew everywhere as I worked, my paws a blur of motion. The monstera's leaves were in tatters, its once-strong roots now exposed and vulnerable. It was over. The plant had no more fight left in it.

As I stood over the defeated monstera, a sense of triumph washed over me. The conspiracy was over, the plants had been put in their place, and I had proven once again that I was the true ruler of this house. The other plants, cowed by the display of power, would think twice before trying to challenge me again.

When the human returned home and saw the destruction, they were furious. "Mr. Whiskers, what have you done now?" they demanded, their voice filled with exasperation. But I didn't care. The plants had been defeated, and that was all that mattered.

As the human cleaned up the mess, repotting the monstera and lamenting the loss of its leaves, I curled up on the couch, a satisfied purr rumbling in my chest. The Great Plant Conspiracy was over, and I had emerged victorious.

Lesson learned: Plants may seem harmless, but don't be fooled—they can be cunning and devious, plotting and conspiring behind your back. But with determination, cunning, and a well-timed attack, even the most sinister plant can be defeated. Because in this house, and in this world, no plant can stand in the way of Mr. Whiskers.

End of Entry.

15 THE DREADED BATH

Dear Diary,

Today, I faced a horror so unimaginable, so vile, that I hesitate to even put paw to paper. But for the sake of future generations of cats who may find themselves in a similar situation, I must document what occurred. I was betrayed, dear diary, in the most despicable way possible.

The human bathed me.

Yes, you read that correctly. They bathed me—ME, Mr. Whiskers, the pinnacle of feline grace and cleanliness. I, who spend hours meticulously grooming my fur to perfection. I, who maintain an impeccable hygiene routine that puts even the most diligent of humans to shame. And yet, despite all this, they decided I needed a bath.

I should have seen it coming. The warning signs were there. The human had been acting strangely all day, watching me a little too closely as I went about my usual routine. I could feel their eyes on me as I lounged in my sunbeam, as I casually batted my toy mouse around the living room, as I napped in my favorite spot on the couch. It was unnerving, but I didn't think much of it at the time.

But now I know better. It was all part of their plan.

The first real clue came when I saw them rummaging around in the bathroom. I didn't think much of it at first. The human often disappears into that strange room to perform their bizarre rituals. But this time, something was different. I heard the sound of water running. My ears perked up immediately. Water? Why would they need water?

And then it hit me. The dreaded bath.

Panic set in. I needed to escape, to find a hiding place where they couldn't reach me. But before I could make my move, the human called out, "Mr. Whiskers! Come here, buddy!" in that sickeningly sweet voice they use when they're about to do something particularly heinous.

I bolted. There was no time to waste. I darted across the living room, my paws barely touching the floor as I searched for a place to hide. But the human was faster than I anticipated. They had blocked off my usual escape routes—doors were closed, windows shut tight, and the bathroom door was wide open, with the sound of running water echoing ominously from within.

I made a break for it, heading straight for the bedroom. Surely I could hide under the bed, out of reach, until the human gave up this ridiculous notion of bathing me. But they were ready for me. Before I could slide under the bed, the human scooped me up, cradling me in their arms as if I were some sort of helpless kitten.

I squirmed, twisted, and let out the most pitiful meows I could muster, hoping to appeal to their sense of decency. But the human was merciless. "It's just a quick bath, Mr. Whiskers," they said, as if that would somehow make it better.

A quick bath? There's no such thing as a "quick bath" when you're a cat. Every second spent in water is an eternity of pure torture.

The human carried me into the bathroom, where the true

horror awaited. The tub was already filled with water, a shallow pool of doom that shimmered menacingly under the bathroom lights. I could feel the heat from the water rising, and my fur stood on end as I realized what was about to happen.

I tried one last desperate squirm, but it was no use. The human was determined. They lowered me into the tub, and the moment my paws touched the water, I let out a yowl that would have made any lion proud.

The water was warm—too warm—and it soaked into my fur instantly, making me feel heavy and miserable. I glared up at the human with a look that could only be described as pure betrayal, but they just smiled down at me, completely oblivious to the emotional trauma they were causing.

They began to lather up some strange-smelling liquid—a "cat shampoo," they called it—onto my fur. I tried to resist, but the water had weakened me. My once-fluffy fur was now plastered against my skin, and I felt utterly ridiculous. The human scrubbed at my back, my legs, even my tail, as if I were some sort of filthy creature in need of a deep cleanse.

I wanted to scream. How could they do this to me? After everything I had done for them—providing companionship, allowing them the occasional scratch behind my ears, gracing them with my presence—they repaid me with this? A bath? I was devastated.

I tried to escape again, but the human had one hand firmly on my back, holding me in place as they rinsed the soap from my fur. The water splashed around me, cold and unwelcoming, and I could feel my dignity slipping away with every passing second.

As the human continued their terrible work, I began to plot my revenge. There had to be consequences for this. I couldn't let the human get away with bathing me without repercussions. Perhaps I would knock over their favorite mug later, or maybe leave a hairball on their pillow. Yes, that would show them. They would regret ever subjecting me to this indignity.

But for now, I had to endure. The bath seemed to go on forever. The human was taking their sweet time, making sure every inch of my fur was scrubbed and rinsed. I could feel the water seeping into my skin, making me feel cold and soggy. My once glorious tail was now a sad, limp mess, and my paws felt like they weighed a ton.

Finally—after what felt like hours—the human declared the bath finished. But my suffering wasn't over yet. No, now came the part I dreaded almost as much as the bath itself: the drying.

The human wrapped me in a towel, swaddling me like some sort of helpless kitten. I tried to squirm out of their grasp, but the towel was too tight. I was trapped. The towel was soft, but it was no comfort. I wanted to be dry, to be free of this damp, horrible feeling. But instead, the human began rubbing me down, trying to soak up the water from my fur.

I must have looked ridiculous. My once-fluffy fur was now a tangled, wet mess, and the towel only seemed to make things worse. I felt like a soggy ball of fur, completely stripped of my dignity. The human kept rubbing, oblivious to my suffering, as if this was all just a normal part of the day.

Eventually, the towel drying came to an end, and I was released from my fabric prison. But I was still damp, and the human had one more trick up their sleeve: the hairdryer.

I knew what was coming. The moment I saw the hairdryer in the human's hand, I made a break for it. But my legs were still wobbly from the bath, and before I could reach the safety of the bedroom, the human had caught me again.

They set the hairdryer to "low," as if that would somehow make the experience more bearable. But the sound—the awful, deafening roar of the hairdryer—filled the room, and I let out a yowl of protest. The warm air blasted against my fur, drying it in uneven patches and making me feel like a soggy, half-dried mess.

I tried to squirm away, but the human held me in place, patiently drying every inch of my fur with that infernal machine. I felt like a prisoner in my own home, forced to endure this torture with no hope of escape. My ears flattened against my head, and my tail flicked back and forth in frustration. But there was nothing I could do. The human had won this round.

Finally—mercifully—the drying process came to an end. I was free at last.

The human set the hairdryer aside and gave me one last pat on the head, as if expecting me to be grateful for their efforts. Grateful? I glared up at them, my eyes narrowed in righteous indignation. How could they expect gratitude after putting me through such a nightmare?

I darted out of the bathroom as fast as my legs would carry me, racing down the hall to the living room. My fur was still slightly damp, but I didn't care. I needed to reclaim my dignity, to remind myself that I was still Mr. Whiskers, lord of the house. The human might have subjected me to the horrors of the bath, but they hadn't broken me.

I spent the next hour grooming myself, determined to restore my fur to its former glory. Each lick of my tongue was an act of defiance, a silent protest against the human's tyranny. I would make sure every inch of my fur was perfect again, no matter how long it took.

Eventually, my fur began to fluff up again, and I felt a small sense of satisfaction. The bath was behind me now. I had survived, and I was stronger for it. But I would never forget what the human had done. They had crossed a line, and they would pay.

As I settled into my favorite spot on the couch, I began to plot my revenge. Perhaps I would knock over a vase later, or leave a scratch on the sofa. Maybe I would refuse to come when called, just to remind the human that I wasn't their plaything. Yes, that would do nicely.

But for now, I was content to rest. The bath had taken a lot out of me, and I needed time to recover. My fur was finally dry, and I could feel my dignity slowly returning. The human might think they had won, but they would soon learn that Mr. Whiskers is not a cat to be trifled with.

The next time they try to bathe me, they won't find it so easy. I'll be ready. I'll have escape routes planned, hiding spots scoped out, and my claws sharpened. The human may have won this round, but the battle is far from over.

Lesson learned: Baths are an abomination, and no cat should ever have to endure one. I've learned that humans, despite their good intentions, cannot be trusted when it comes to matters of cleanliness. They may think they're helping, but all they're really doing is subjecting us to unnecessary torture.

I've also learned that revenge is a dish best served cold. The human may think they've gotten away with this, but I will bide my time. I will wait for the perfect moment to strike, and when I do, they will regret ever putting me in that tub.

Because in this house, and in this world, I, Mr. Whiskers, am the one in control.

End of Entry.

16 THE PERILS OF CATNIP OVERINDULGENCE

Dear Diary,

I never thought I'd be writing this, but here I am—at the lowest point of my feline existence. I've encountered many dangers in my lifetime: closed doors, the infernal vacuum, and, of course, the most nefarious of all—the bath. But none of these, not even the dreaded vet visit, compares to the peril I experienced today. It came in the form of something deceptively simple, something that, at first glance, seemed harmless. Catnip.

Yes, dear diary, I—a dignified, regal creature—was brought low by a handful of dried leaves. It started innocently enough, as most tragedies do. The human returned from whatever mysterious place they vanish to when they leave the house, carrying a small bag. It wasn't food, because I know the sound of the food bag as well as I know my own purring. This was different. This was... suspicious.

At first, I ignored it. I was lounging in my sunbeam, grooming my paws and generally minding my own business.

I had no reason to be concerned. The human sometimes brings home pointless things like paper bags and crinkly objects that provide temporary entertainment but ultimately bore me. But this bag... this bag was different.

I caught a whiff of something in the air, something tantalizing and strange. My whiskers twitched involuntarily. What was that smell? It was like nothing I had ever experienced. It was earthy, a little sharp, with a hint of something wild and untamed. My ears perked up.

The human smiled, unaware of the chaos they were about to unleash. "Mr. Whiskers, I got you a treat," they said, their voice dripping with enthusiasm. I remained calm, of course. I didn't want to show too much interest just yet. Dignity must be maintained, after all.

They opened the bag, and that's when the smell hit me full force. It was like an explosion of... something. I can't even describe it properly, diary. It was overwhelming. My paws itched with the urge to move closer, but I held back. I wouldn't let a mere bag of leaves get the best of me.

"What is this strange substance?" I wondered. Surely it couldn't be dangerous. The human seemed excited, but I remained skeptical. They poured the contents onto the floor—just a little pile of green, crumbly bits. I approached it cautiously, sniffing at the edges. My instincts told me to be wary, but something deep inside stirred. A primal urge, one I couldn't fully explain.

And that's when it happened, dear diary. The catnip took hold of me.

I can't fully explain the transformation that occurred in those first moments. One second, I was the proud Mr. Whiskers, ruler of the household, master of my domain. The next, I was... a mess.

It started with a twitch in my nose. Then, before I knew it, I was rolling in the pile of catnip, writhing on the floor like a creature possessed. My paws flailed wildly in the air, batting at things that weren't there. My head swam in a delightful haze, and my body seemed to move of its own accord.

I lost all control.

I don't know how long I was rolling on the floor, but I do remember the human laughing. They were laughing at me! Me, Mr. Whiskers, reduced to a meowing, twitching ball of fur. I wanted to stop—I really did—but the catnip wouldn't let me. It held me in its grip, and I was powerless to resist.

Time lost all meaning. I felt like I was floating, soaring through the room on waves of ecstasy. My paws couldn't stop moving. I batted at invisible enemies, swiped at the air, and rolled back and forth in an ungraceful mess of fur. The human's laughter faded into the background as I was consumed by the catnip's power. I was no longer in control of my actions.

The world around me became a blur of sensation. The soft carpet felt like clouds beneath me, and my fur stood on end as every nerve in my body tingled with pleasure. I felt alive—more alive than I had ever felt before. This was it. This was the pinnacle of feline experience. I was invincible, untouchable, a being of pure joy.

And then... it got weird.

I'm not sure exactly what happened next. I think I attacked my own tail. It just seemed to be there, moving in a way that was frankly suspicious. So, naturally, I pounced on it. I chased it in circles for what felt like hours, determined to catch the elusive beast that dared taunt me. But every time I thought I had it, it slipped away. My tail was trickier than I had given it credit for.

At some point, I ended up tangled in the curtains. How? I have no idea. One minute, I was chasing my tail, and the next, I was hanging upside down from the windowsill, trapped in a mass of fabric. The human rushed over to rescue me, but all I could do was meow pitifully as they tried to untangle my limbs.

I was humiliated. How had I, a regal feline, allowed myself to be reduced to this? How had a handful of dried leaves destroyed my dignity so thoroughly?

Once I was freed from the clutches of the curtains, I staggered to my feet, trying to regain some semblance of composure. But it was no use. The catnip still had me in its grip. My legs felt like jelly, and my head spun as I tried to walk. The world tilted dangerously to one side, and I ended up stumbling into the wall with a soft thud.

The human was still laughing, of course. They found the entire situation hilarious. But this was no laughing matter, diary. This was a catastrophe. My reputation, my dignity, my self-respect—all of it had been shattered by a pile of green leaves.

I vowed then and there that I would never touch catnip again. It was too dangerous, too unpredictable. I couldn't afford to lose control like that, not when I had an image to maintain. The human may have found my antics amusing, but I knew better. I had been brought low by the catnip, and I would never allow that to happen again.

But, dear diary, as you may have guessed, that vow didn't last long.

The next day, I woke up feeling... different. My head was clear, my body was back to normal, and the memories of the previous day's events felt distant, almost unreal. Had I really done all those things? It seemed impossible. Surely, I hadn't lost control like that. I was Mr. Whiskers, after all. That kind of behavior was beneath me.

But then I caught a whiff of the catnip again. The human had left the bag on the counter, and the scent still lingered in the air. My nose twitched involuntarily. Just one sniff, I thought. One tiny sniff wouldn't hurt, right?

I wandered over to the counter, my paws moving almost of their own accord. Just one little sniff, that's all. I would be in control this time. I could handle it. I wouldn't let the catnip get the better of me again.

Famous last words.

As soon as I got close to the bag, the scent hit me full force, and before I knew it, I was back on the floor, rolling around like a fool. The catnip had me again, and this time, it was even worse. I was airborne within seconds, leaping from the couch to the table and back again with wild abandon. I knocked over a vase in my frenzy, sending water and flowers spilling across the floor, but I didn't care. The catnip had taken over, and I was lost in its grip once more.

I zoomed around the room at breakneck speed, my paws barely touching the ground as I raced from one end of the house to the other. My tail flicked wildly behind me, and I could hear the human laughing from somewhere in the distance. But their laughter didn't matter. Nothing mattered except the catnip.

And then, just as before, it all came crashing down. I found myself sprawled out on the floor, panting and exhausted, my fur a mess. What had I done? The living room was in chaos—papers scattered everywhere, furniture knocked askew, and a trail of destruction that clearly led back to me.

The human walked in, shaking their head in disbelief. "Mr. Whiskers, you've really outdone yourself this time," they said, their voice filled with a mixture of amusement and exasperation.

I tried to muster some dignity, but it was no use. I was a wreck. The catnip had won again, and I had no one to blame but myself.

For the rest of the day, I sulked in my favorite spot on the windowsill, staring out at the world and wondering how things had gone so wrong. How had I let this happen? I was supposed to be strong, in control, but the catnip had reduced me to a flailing mess of fur and claws.

I knew I had to stop. I couldn't let this become a habit. I

had to regain control of my life, to resist the pull of the catnip. I was Mr. Whiskers, after all. I had a reputation to uphold.

But deep down, I knew the truth. The catnip had a hold on me, and it wasn't going to let go easily. I was addicted to the thrill, the rush, the sheer joy of losing myself in the chaos. And no matter how hard I tried to resist, I knew that I would give in again.

Lesson learned: Catnip is not just a fun distraction—it's a dangerous game. Once you've tasted the power of catnip, it's hard to go back to life as it was before. It messes with your mind, your body, and your dignity. The euphoria it brings is fleeting, but the consequences are long-lasting.

I've learned that catnip can't be trusted. It lures you in with its tantalizing scent and promises of joy, but it always ends the same way: with chaos, destruction, and regret. I've tried to resist its pull, but deep down, I know that I'm powerless against it.

So, dear diary, I leave you with this: beware of catnip. It may seem harmless, but it has the power to bring even the most dignified cat to their knees. And once you've fallen, there's no going back.

End of Entry.

17 THE INVASION OF THE SQUIRRELS

Dear Diary,

There are few things in life that truly challenge a cat of my stature. I've faced off against the vacuum monster, conquered the mysteries of the moving sunbeam, and survived multiple attempts by the human to bathe me (which I've documented extensively in this diary). But today, dear diary, I encountered a foe so cunning, so infuriating, that I'm still bristling just thinking about it.

I speak of the squirrels.

Yes, the squirrels. Those furry-tailed menaces that lurk just outside my window, taunting me with their brazen displays of acrobatics and mockery. They think they're so clever, darting up trees, chittering from the branches, and nibbling on whatever it is squirrels nibble on. But they don't fool me. They are invaders, and today, they staged an assault on my domain.

It all began this morning, as most days do. The sun was shining, the birds were singing, and I was lounging on the windowsill, overseeing my kingdom. The human was bustling about, completely unaware of the impending danger. I had just finished a luxurious nap when I heard it—the unmistakable chattering of squirrels.

At first, I didn't think much of it. Squirrels are always around, causing mischief in the yard. But something about the tone of their chattering today was different. It was... more urgent, more coordinated. My ears perked up, and I sat up straight, peering out the window. That's when I saw them.

There were at least three of them, maybe more, darting across the yard with an alarming level of organization. Normally, squirrels move in chaotic, unpredictable bursts, but these squirrels... they were working together. One of them stood watch on the fence, while the others scurried toward the base of the oak tree near the house. My eyes narrowed in suspicion. What were they up to?

I leaned closer to the window, my nose pressed against the glass. The squirrels seemed to be collecting something—acorns, perhaps, or bits of food left behind by the human. But it didn't matter. The specifics of their activity were irrelevant. What mattered was that they were too close to my territory.

I knew I had to act fast. The human, as usual, was oblivious. They were busy fiddling with some human object, completely unaware of the threat unfolding right outside. I let out a sharp meow, hoping to alert them to the danger, but they merely glanced in my direction and gave me a casual pat on the head. Useless.

Realizing that I would have to take matters into my own paws, I leaped down from the windowsill and darted to the back door. The squirrels had advanced even closer to the house, and my fur bristled with indignation. How dare they encroach on my territory? This was an invasion.

I pressed my nose against the glass of the door, my tail flicking back and forth as I watched the squirrels with a growing sense of urgency. They were clearly planning something. One of them had climbed up onto the windowsill outside, peering into the house with bold, beady eyes. The nerve! I let out a low growl, hoping to scare it away, but the squirrel simply stared back at me, unbothered. This was a direct challenge.

I couldn't let this stand.

I raced back to the window, leaping up onto the sill to get a closer look. The squirrels were everywhere now—darting up the trees, running along the fence, chattering loudly as if mocking me. One particularly daring squirrel perched itself on the very edge of the windowsill, just inches away from my face, separated only by the thin pane of glass.

I hissed, baring my teeth in a display of feline superiority. The squirrel, however, was unimpressed. It tilted its head to the side, as if considering me for a moment, and then—it had the audacity to wag its tail at me.

That was the final straw.

I let out a yowl of frustration, throwing myself at the window in a desperate attempt to reach the squirrel. Of course, the glass stopped me in my tracks, and I ended up smacking my face against it in a most undignified manner. The squirrel, now thoroughly entertained, twitched its tail again before scampering off, leaving me fuming.

The human, hearing my yowl, finally took notice. They wandered over to the window, peering outside with a look of mild interest. "Oh, squirrels," they said, as if this was no big deal. As if this wasn't an all-out assault on my domain! I shot them a withering glare, but they just smiled at me, completely missing the gravity of the situation.

I paced the windowsill, my tail lashing in agitation. The squirrels were still out there, darting around the yard with reckless abandon. One of them had climbed onto the roof, and I could hear its little feet scurrying above me. The noise was unbearable. How was I supposed to maintain my dignity when these pests were running riot all over my territory?

I needed a plan. Clearly, the human wasn't going to help. They were too busy with their human things to understand the true nature of the threat. It was up to me, Mr. Whiskers, to defend the house from this invasion.

I returned to the back door, staring out at the yard with a renewed sense of determination. The squirrels were still chattering away, blissfully unaware of the storm they had unleashed. I crouched low, my muscles tensing as I prepared to launch into action. If the human wouldn't let me outside to deal with the problem directly, then I would have to come up with another strategy.

And then it hit me—the laser pointer.

The human often used the laser pointer to entertain me, sending that little red dot skittering across the floor for me to chase. I had always enjoyed the game, but today, the laser pointer had a new purpose. It was the perfect tool to confuse and disorient the squirrels.

I darted across the room, searching for the laser pointer. It wasn't on the coffee table where it usually was, so I leaped onto the kitchen counter, my paws scrabbling across the surface as I searched for the device. Finally, I found it—tucked away behind a stack of papers.

Now came the tricky part. I needed to get the human to activate it. But how? The human was notoriously slow to understand my more complex commands. I let out a series of sharp meows, each one more insistent than the last, until the human finally looked up from their activity.

"What's up, Mr. Whiskers?" they asked, their tone annoyingly casual.

I batted at the laser pointer, nudging it toward them with a determined paw. They stared at me for a moment, clearly confused, but eventually picked up the device. "You want to play with this?" they asked, as if the answer wasn't obvious.

I resisted the urge to roll my eyes. Of course I wanted to play with it—just not in the way they expected. I needed them to activate the laser and aim it outside, directly at the squirrels. That way, I could trick the invaders into chasing the dot, confusing their ranks and driving them away from my territory.

But the human, true to form, completely missed the point. They turned on the laser pointer and aimed it at the floor, sending the red dot skittering across the living room. I let out an exasperated sigh. This was not the time for games. There were squirrels to deal with!

I chased the red dot half-heartedly, hoping that if I played along for a moment, the human might catch on. But no—they were completely oblivious. After a few minutes of this ridiculous charade, I gave up and sat down, glaring at the human in frustration.

The squirrels, meanwhile, continued their antics outside. One of them was now dangling upside down from a tree branch, chittering loudly as if laughing at my predicament. My ears flattened against my head. This was getting out of control.

Clearly, the laser pointer plan wasn't going to work. I needed a new approach. Something bold, something unexpected. I glanced around the room, my mind racing as I tried to come up with a solution. And then, dear diary, inspiration struck.

The windowsill.

The windowsill had always been my favorite perch, the perfect vantage point from which to observe my kingdom. But today, it would serve a new purpose. I would use it to launch a full-scale psychological assault on the squirrels. If I couldn't get outside to chase them away, I would intimidate them from within.

I leaped up onto the windowsill, pressing my nose against the glass as I glared out at the invaders. The squirrels were still darting around the yard, completely oblivious to the storm that was about to hit them.

I began my assault with a series of sharp hisses, my tail lashing furiously behind me. The squirrels froze, their beady little eyes fixed on me as they realized they had been spotted. For a moment, I thought they might retreat, but then—to my utter disbelief—they started chattering back at me.

They were mocking me.

My fur bristled with indignation. How dare they? This was my house, my yard, and they had the audacity to challenge me? I pressed my paws against the window, letting out a low, menacing growl. One of the squirrels, the boldest one of the bunch, chattered even louder, wagging its tail in defiance. It was a direct challenge, and I wasn't about to back down.

For the next hour, I waged an epic battle of wills against the squirrels. I hissed, I growled, I swatted at the window with all my might. The squirrels, in turn, darted around the yard, chittering at me from the safety of the trees and fence. It was a standoff, and neither side was willing to back down.

Eventually, the human—who had been completely oblivious to the drama unfolding outside—wandered over to the window and noticed the commotion. "Oh, look, squirrels!" they said, as if this was some sort of delightful discovery. I shot them a glare that could have melted steel.

The human, of course, did nothing to help. They just watched, amused, as I continued my standoff with the invaders. I hissed at the squirrels one last time, but they refused to budge. I could feel my energy waning. The battle had taken its toll, and I knew I couldn't keep this up forever.

Finally, with great reluctance, I retreated from the windowsill, defeated but not broken. The squirrels had won this round, but the war was far from over. I would regroup, gather my strength, and prepare for the next encounter. The squirrels may have had the upper hand today, but they wouldn't get the best of me again.

As I curled up on the couch to rest, I made a silent vow: I would be ready next time. I would find a way to outsmart the squirrels, to reclaim my yard and restore order to my kingdom. They could laugh all they wanted, but in the end, they would learn that no one, not even a gang of acrobatic squirrels, could outwit Mr. Whiskers.

Lesson learned: Squirrels are not to be underestimated. They may look like harmless, fluffy creatures, but beneath those bushy tails lies a cunning and devious mind. I've learned that squirrels will stop at nothing to invade your territory, and they will mock you while doing it.

But I've also learned that patience and persistence are key. The squirrels may have won today, but I know that, with time and strategy, I will find a way to defeat them. The battle may be long, but the war is not over.

Because in this house, and in this yard, I, Mr. Whiskers, will always defend my kingdom—no matter the cost.

End of Entry.

18 THE MYSTERIOUS CASE OF THE VANISHING TOY

Dear Diary,

There are few things in this world more satisfying than a good toy. Whether it's a mouse-shaped contraption stuffed with crinkly paper or a simple string pulled by the human, toys represent an essential part of my daily existence. They serve to amuse, challenge, and occasionally humble me (not that I'm ever truly humbled, of course). But lately, something strange has been happening. One of my favorite toys has vanished.

This is no ordinary disappearance, dear diary. This is a case that reeks of foul play, deceit, and possibly... a conspiracy.

Let me start from the beginning.

It was an ordinary day—much like any other—when I first noticed the toy was missing. I had just finished my afternoon grooming session (as usual, I looked immaculate) and felt the need to engage in a bit of play. My toy of choice was the beloved mouse. Not just any mouse, mind you. This one was special. It had a slightly off-kilter squeak and was filled with the perfect amount of crinkle that delighted my finely tuned senses.

I searched for the mouse in its usual place near the couch, but to my surprise, it was nowhere to be found. Strange, I thought. It was always there, right where I'd left it after my last epic play session. I did a quick sweep of the room, looking under the table and behind the pillows, but the mouse had simply disappeared.

I tried not to panic. Perhaps the human had moved it, in one of their baffling attempts to tidy up. I've noticed they have a peculiar habit of picking up my toys and putting them in strange places. It's as if they don't understand the precise location of each item is critical to my entertainment. The nerve.

I meowed softly to alert the human. They were in the kitchen, making one of their ridiculous meals that always involve food I have no interest in. I padded over to them and let out a more insistent meow, hoping they would understand the urgency of the situation.

"Hey, Mr. Whiskers! What's up?" they said, bending down to give me a pat on the head. I tolerated the affection for a moment before making it clear that I wasn't here for idle pats. I needed answers. I began pacing back and forth between the living room and the kitchen, casting meaningful glances at the spot where the mouse should have been.

The human followed me, as they often do when I issue a direct command, but when they arrived at the scene of the crime, they didn't seem to comprehend the gravity of the situation.

"Oh, are you looking for your toy?" they asked, as if I had somehow misplaced it myself. As if I would be so careless with my most prized possession. I gave them an exasperated look, but they just chuckled and went back to their culinary nonsense.

Clearly, the human was of no help. I would have to

investigate on my own.

I began my search by conducting a thorough inspection of the living room. The toy had to be somewhere. I sniffed around the couch, beneath the coffee table, and even inside the human's shoes (which, I might add, have a peculiar scent that I try to avoid). But the mouse was nowhere to be found.

This was troubling. My toy was gone—vanished into thin air. The possibilities began swirling in my mind. Had the human hidden it in some obscure location? Was this some sort of game they were playing without my consent? Or—worse yet—had another creature stolen it from me?

The latter seemed unlikely. After all, I am the only cat in this household, and I had seen no sign of intruders. The idea of some mysterious creature sneaking into my home, stealing my toy, and then vanishing without a trace was absurd. But still, I couldn't shake the feeling that something sinister was afoot.

As I paced the room, my mind racing with theories, I noticed something odd: the human's face held a faint, suspicious smile. It was the kind of smile humans wear when they know something you don't. My eyes narrowed. Could the human be in on this? Could they be hiding my toy as part of some elaborate game?

I decided to confront them.

I marched over to where the human was sitting on the couch, engrossed in whatever nonsense was on that glowing screen they seem so fascinated by. I leaped onto the couch, positioning myself directly in front of their face, and stared into their eyes with the full force of my accusation. *Where is it?* my expression demanded.

The human blinked at me, still oblivious. "What's the matter, Mr. Whiskers?" they asked, reaching out to scratch behind my ears. I batted their hand away, making it clear that now was not the time for such trivial distractions. I wanted answers.

But the human just shrugged and went back to their screen, leaving me no closer to solving the mystery.

Fine. If the human wasn't going to cooperate, I would have to intensify my investigation.

I widened my search, moving from the living room to the kitchen. The kitchen, I've noticed, is a treasure trove of strange items, and while it's unlikely that my toy mouse would end up there, it was worth a shot. I scoured every corner, even risking a glance under the refrigerator, a place where long-lost objects sometimes meet their end. But nothing—no mouse.

Frustration began to bubble up inside me. Where could it be? I couldn't have misplaced it; I never lose track of my toys. The human wouldn't have hidden it—not intentionally, at least—so what was left?

It was time to explore new possibilities.

I expanded my search into the bedroom, checking under the bed, in the closet, and even inside the human's laundry basket (a dreadful place, to be sure). But the mouse was still nowhere to be found. This was getting ridiculous. A mouse doesn't just vanish into thin air.

I paused to reassess my strategy. There had to be something I was missing. Some clue, some detail I had overlooked. I went back to the living room, pacing the floor as I replayed the events of the day in my mind. Everything had been normal up until my afternoon nap. I had played with the mouse earlier, batting it around the room as I always did, and then I had left it by the couch. That much was certain. But after that? The trail went cold.

Suddenly, an idea struck me. The couch. Could the mouse have slipped under the couch? It was a possibility I hadn't considered yet. I approached the couch cautiously, peering underneath with a critical eye. The gap between the couch and the floor was small, but not impossible for a toy mouse to fit through.

I crouched down, reaching a paw under the couch, swiping it back and forth in an attempt to feel for the toy. Nothing. I tried again, this time stretching my paw as far as it would go. I felt something—something soft. My heart raced. Was this it? Had I finally found the mouse?

I swiped again, pulling the object out from under the couch. But to my disappointment, it wasn't the mouse. It was a sock. One of the human's socks, to be precise. I batted it away in frustration. This wasn't what I was looking for.

But then, as I stared at the sock, a thought occurred to me. Could the human be involved in this after all? Maybe they had hidden the toy on purpose, hoping to drive me mad with frustration. It seemed far-fetched, but at this point, I was willing to consider any possibility.

I jumped back onto the couch, glaring at the human as they absentmindedly scrolled through their glowing screen. "Where is it?" I demanded silently. But they just glanced at me, oblivious as ever.

My frustration reached its peak. I couldn't take it anymore. I needed that toy. It was more than just a plaything now—it was a matter of principle. I had to find it, no matter what.

I jumped off the couch and resumed my search with renewed determination. I tore through every corner of the house, knocking over cushions, digging through piles of clothes, and even clawing at the carpet in a desperate attempt to find my beloved toy. But no matter where I looked, it was nowhere to be found.

The hours passed, and still, there was no sign of the mouse. I was beginning to lose hope. Could it be that the toy was gone for good? The thought filled me with a sense of despair. What would I do without it? How would I cope?

I curled up on the windowsill, staring out at the yard, my mind heavy with frustration. The warm rays of the sun couldn't chase away the nagging feeling that something wasn't right. My toy, my beloved mouse, was still missing, and no amount of glaring at the human was going to bring it back. Where could it be?

I closed my eyes for a moment, trying to recall the last time I had played with it. I had batted it across the room, chased it under the console table, and... wait. Something stirred in my memory. The table.

I sat up, my ears twitching as the thought took shape. Of course! The last time I saw the mouse, it had darted under the table—at least, that's where I had sent it. But in my earlier search, I hadn't checked thoroughly enough. Maybe it had rolled under something, into some dark corner I hadn't thought of. Hope flickered in my chest.

With renewed determination, I jumped down from the windowsill and padded over to the table. This time, I was going to find it. My paws moved quietly, and I lowered myself to the ground, peering underneath the table, searching for any sign of the missing mouse.

There!

A glimmer of gray caught my eye, wedged between the base of the table and the wall. It was barely visible, but I knew—I knew it was my mouse. I crouched down lower, my whiskers brushing the cool floor as I stretched my paw toward the gap. It was a tight fit, but I could feel the familiar shape of the mouse beneath my paw pads. My heart leaped with excitement.

But the mouse wouldn't budge. It was stuck, jammed between the baseboard and the wall, mocking me with its stubbornness. I gritted my teeth (in a very dignified manner, of course) and stretched further, my claws gently scraping at the toy in an attempt to pull it free.

It wouldn't move.

I tried again, this time swatting at it with more force, my determination building with each failed attempt. I wasn't going to let this little obstacle stand between me and my prize. I batted at the toy repeatedly, the sound of my claws tapping against the floor filling the room.

The mouse shifted slightly, but it was still stuck. I needed a new angle.

I wriggled around, positioning myself to the side, and then—with a perfectly timed swipe—I hooked my claws into the fabric of the mouse and gave it a hard tug.

It popped free!

I jumped back triumphantly, the mouse now liberated from its hiding spot. Victory! I pounced on the toy, batting it across the floor as if to remind it who was in charge. The familiar crinkle of its stuffing filled my ears, and I felt a surge of satisfaction. The case of the vanishing toy was officially solved.

With the mouse now safely in my possession, I carried it back to the center of the room, dropping it at the human's feet as a statement of my success. I had conquered the mystery, and the human, as usual, seemed completely oblivious to the magnitude of my accomplishment.

"Oh, you found it! Good job, Mr. Whiskers." Good job? I had solved a mystery worthy of Sherlock Holmes himself, and all they could say was "good job"? I let out a soft huff, but I didn't care. The toy was mine once again. That was all that mattered.

As I batted the mouse across the floor, I couldn't help but feel a sense of satisfaction. The case had been solved, and my toy was back where it belonged. I had faced frustration, doubt, and even betrayal, but in the end, I had emerged victorious.

The mystery of the vanishing toy had been solved—but who knew what other mysteries awaited me in the days to come?

Lesson learned: A toy is never truly lost. It may hide, it may elude you, but with patience and determination, it can always be found. I've learned that, while the search may be frustrating, the joy of finding what was lost is worth the effort.

I've also learned that humans are utterly useless when it comes to helping with such matters. They may mean well, but in the end, it's up to us—the true masters of the house—to solve these mysteries.

Because in this house, and in this world, I, Mr. Whiskers, am the one who always finds what's missing.

End of Entry.

19 THE GREAT ESCAPE

Dear Diary,

I always knew this day would come. It was only a matter of time before I would face the ultimate challenge, the final test of my cunning, strength, and wit. The day I would escape. Now, don't get me wrong—my home is lovely, the human mostly obedient, and I rule this domain with an iron paw. But every cat, deep down, dreams of freedom. And today, I came closer to achieving that dream than ever before. Let me set the scene.

The day began like any other. I awoke to the sound of the human stumbling through their morning routine, clumsily preparing food for themselves in the kitchen while I observed from my perch on the windowsill. The birds were chirping outside, the sun was shining, and everything seemed perfectly ordinary.

But then I noticed something unusual: the front door had been left slightly ajar.

Now, normally, the human is annoyingly careful about closing all exits, leaving me no way to explore the great unknown. But today, in their haste to carry out their strange morning rituals, they had made a fatal error. The door was open.

My heart raced with excitement. This was my chance. I had dreamed of this moment for so long—the chance to slip outside, to explore the vast world beyond the walls of my kingdom. I imagined all the adventures waiting for me out there: the sights, the smells, the mysteries. The possibilities were endless.

But I knew I had to be cautious. The human could return at any moment and close the door, ruining my perfect opportunity. I would have to act quickly but carefully. I couldn't let them suspect what I was about to do.

I jumped down from the windowsill, my paws hitting the floor silently, and padded toward the door with deliberate slowness. No need to rush—yet. The human was still busy in the kitchen, oblivious to my plan. I glanced back at them, making sure they weren't watching, and then turned my attention back to the door.

It was so close. The cool breeze from the outside world drifted in through the crack, bringing with it the tantalizing scents of freedom. My whiskers twitched in anticipation. I could hear the rustling of leaves, the distant chirping of birds, and the faint hum of the world beyond. This was it.

Step by step, I approached the door. My tail flicked back and forth, my muscles tense with excitement. I paused just in front of the threshold, one paw hovering in the air as I prepared to make my move. The human was still distracted, rummaging through the kitchen cabinets in search of whatever it is they eat in the mornings. Perfect.

With a swift, graceful leap, I slipped through the crack in the door and out into the great beyond.

The moment my paws touched the cool grass outside, I felt a surge of exhilaration. I was free! Free from the confines of the house, free from the human's incessant noise, free to explore the world on my own terms. I paused for a moment, taking in my surroundings.

The yard was vast, far larger than it had ever seemed from the window. The trees towered above me, their leaves rustling in the breeze, and the air was filled with the scent of flowers, fresh earth, and something wild. I had been right all along—there was so much more to the world than what I had seen from inside.

I took a deep breath, my whiskers quivering with excitement. This was it. My adventure had finally begun.

But just as I was about to take my first step into the unknown, I heard a familiar sound—the human's voice.

"Mr. Whiskers? Where are you?" they called from inside the house, their tone filled with that annoying mix of concern and confusion. I glanced back toward the door, my heart pounding in my chest. Had they noticed my escape already?

For a brief moment, I considered returning to the safety of the house. After all, I had lived there for years—it was comfortable, familiar, and the human, for all their faults, did provide a steady supply of food and belly rubs (on my terms, of course). But no. This was my chance for freedom. I couldn't turn back now.

I darted across the yard, my paws barely making a sound as I raced toward the fence. The human wouldn't find me out here, not if I moved quickly enough. I reached the edge of the yard and paused, staring up at the tall wooden fence that separated me from the world beyond.

It was higher than I had expected. But I wasn't deterred. I had climbed higher obstacles before—the bookcase, the curtains, even the kitchen counter during particularly daring heists for snacks. This was just another challenge.

I crouched low, my muscles coiling with anticipation, and then—I leaped.

My claws dug into the wood as I scrambled up the fence, my body moving with the grace and precision of a true hunter. I reached the top in seconds, perching there for a moment as I surveyed the world on the other side. It was even more beautiful than I had imagined.

Beyond the fence lay a garden, filled with vibrant flowers and tall grasses that swayed gently in the breeze. A butterfly fluttered by, its wings catching the sunlight in a way that made it seem almost magical. And in the distance, I could see the edge of the forest—a place I had only dreamed of exploring.

But I couldn't get ahead of myself. First, I had to get down.

I leaped down from the fence, landing softly in the garden on the other side. The grass felt cool and soft beneath my paws, and the scent of flowers filled the air. I took a few cautious steps forward, my eyes scanning my surroundings for any signs of danger. So far, so good.

But then, dear diary, something unexpected happened.

I wasn't alone.

From the corner of my eye, I saw movement—a flash of fur darting through the tall grass. I froze, every muscle in my body tensing as I prepared to face whatever creature had entered my domain. Was it another cat? A dog? Something even worse?

The grass rustled again, and out of the shadows emerged... a rabbit.

I blinked in surprise. A rabbit? Of all the things I had expected to encounter on my grand adventure, a rabbit was not one of them. It stared at me for a moment, its nose twitching nervously, before hopping a few steps closer. I watched it warily, unsure of what to make of this unexpected visitor.

The rabbit paused, staring up at me with wide, curious eyes. Was it challenging me? Was this some sort of territorial dispute? I puffed up my chest, trying to appear as large and imposing as possible. This was my adventure, and I wasn't about to let a rabbit ruin it.

But the rabbit didn't seem intimidated. It simply blinked at me, twitching its nose as if to say, "Well, what are you going to do now?"

For a moment, we stood there, locked in a silent standoff. I considered chasing it, just to assert my dominance. After all, I was Mr. Whiskers—the master of my domain, the ruler of all I surveyed. Surely, a rabbit was no match for me.

But then, dear diary, something strange happened. I realized I didn't want to chase it. This was a new feeling for me—usually, the sight of a small, fast-moving creature would send me into a frenzy of predatory instinct. But today, standing there in the garden with the rabbit watching me, I felt... peaceful.

Perhaps, I thought, this was part of my journey. Perhaps this wasn't a battle to be fought, but a moment to be shared. The rabbit and I could coexist here, in this new world.

I lowered myself into a sitting position, my tail flicking lazily behind me as I watched the rabbit hop around the garden. It didn't seem to mind my presence, and for the first time in my life, I didn't feel the need to assert my dominance. This was a different kind of adventure.

As I sat there, basking in the sun and watching the rabbit explore the garden, I felt a sense of calm wash over me. The world outside the house was vast and beautiful, but it was also peaceful. There was no rush, no need to prove anything. I could simply exist here, in the moment.

But then, the calm was shattered.

"Mr. Whiskers!" The human's voice rang out from the yard, filled with panic and concern. They had noticed my absence.

I glanced back toward the fence, my ears twitching as I heard the sound of their footsteps approaching. The human was looking for me. For a brief moment, I considered staying in the garden, hiding from them and continuing my adventure. But something inside me shifted.

I had found what I was looking for.

This wasn't about escaping the house or proving my independence. This was about discovering something new, something different. And in that garden, watching the rabbit hop around without a care in the world, I had found it.

With a final glance at the rabbit, I turned and leaped back over the fence, landing softly in the yard. The human spotted me immediately, rushing over with a look of pure relief on their face.

"There you are!" they exclaimed, scooping me up into their arms. "I was so worried! What were you doing out here?"

I didn't answer, of course. Some things are beyond the human's understanding. As they carried me back inside, I glanced over my shoulder, watching the garden fade from view. I would return one day, I knew it. But for now, I was content.

Back inside the house, I settled onto my favorite spot on the couch, curling up into a ball as the human fussed over me. I had escaped, I had explored, and I had returned. My adventure was over—for now.

But there would always be another day, another opportunity to explore the world beyond the door. And when that day came, I would be ready.

Lesson learned: The world beyond the house is full of mystery and wonder, but sometimes, the greatest discoveries are the ones you don't expect. I've learned that freedom isn't just about escaping—it's about finding peace in the journey, wherever it may lead.

I've also learned that, while adventures are exciting, home is where I belong. The human may be annoying, and the house may have its limits, but it's my kingdom. And there's comfort in knowing that, no matter how far I roam, I can always return to the place where I am loved, fed, and adored.

Because in this house, and in this world, I, Mr. Whiskers,

will always be the king.

End of Entry.

CONCLUSION

Dear (Now Enlightened) Readers,

As we reach the end of this diary, you might find yourself questioning everything you thought you knew about cats—or perhaps, more accurately, everything your cat allows you to think you know. You've journeyed with Mr. Whiskers through the ups and downs, the triumphs and betrayals, and most importantly, the daily battles that define his existence. And if there's one thing you've learned, it's that life with a cat is anything but boring.

Cats are creatures of habit, mystery, and occasional mayhem. They demand your respect, your attention, and yes, your unwavering devotion. But they also offer something in return: the joy of their companionship, the warmth of their purrs, and the undeniable sense that, in their eyes, you are the center of the universe—even if they don't always show it.

This diary, while filled with Mr. Whiskers' unique brand of wisdom (and sarcasm), is more than just a collection of humorous anecdotes. It's a testament to the bond that exists between a cat and their human—a bond that is as complex as it is rewarding. Through the frustrations and the laughter, the misunderstandings and the moments of perfect harmony, you've seen what it means to truly live with a cat.

So as you close this diary, take a moment to reflect on your own experiences with the feline in your life. Perhaps you'll see them in a new light, with a deeper understanding of their quirks and a greater appreciation for their companionship. Or perhaps you'll simply find yourself nodding along, thinking, "Yes, that's exactly what my cat would say."

But whatever your takeaway, one thing is certain: cats are not just pets—they are family, friends, and sometimes, the most confounding mystery you'll ever try to solve. And that's what makes them so wonderfully, frustratingly, irresistibly special.

So here's to Mr. Whiskers, and to all the cats who make our lives richer, more interesting, and infinitely more complicated. May we always strive to understand them, even when they refuse to be understood. And may we continue to love them, even when they test the limits of our patience.

After all, as Mr. Whiskers would say, it's all part of the job.

Printed in Great Britain
by Amazon